THE RULES OF
ROMANCE
BEFORE MARRIAGE

ANSWERS TO 50 QUESTIONS ABOUT
DATING, SEX & PURITY

CALEB & ALI PIERCE

The Rules of Romance Before Marriage
Answers to 50 Questions About Dating, Sex & Purity
by Caleb & Ali Pierce

This book or parts thereof may not be reproduced in part or in whole, in any form, stored in a retrieval system, or transmitted in any form by any means—electronic, mechanical, photocopy, recording, or otherwise—without prior written permission of the publisher, except as provided by United States of America copyright law.

Scripture quotations marked (ESV) are taken from *The Holy Bible, English Standard Version*. Copyright © 2001, 2007, 2011, 2016 by Crossway Bibles, a division of Good News Publishers. Used by permission. All rights reserved.

Scripture quotations marked (NKJV) are taken from the *New King James Version*. Copyright © 1982 by Thomas Nelson, Inc. All rights reserved. Used by permission.

Scripture quotations marked (NLT) are taken from *The Holy Bible, New Living Translation*. Copyright © 1996, 2004, 2007. Used by permission of Tyndale House Publishers Inc., Carol Stream, Illinois 60188. All rights reserved.

Scripture quotations marked (NIV) are taken from *The Holy Bible, New International Version*®. Copyright © 1973, 1978, 1984, 2011 by Biblica, Inc.® Used by permission. All rights reserved worldwide.

Scripture quotations marked (MSG) are taken from *The Message*. Copyright © 1993, 1994, 1995, 1996, 2000, 2001, 2002. Used by permission of NavPress Publishing Group.

Scripture quotations marked (HCSB) are taken from the *Holman Christian Standard Bible*®. Copyright © 1999, 2000, 2002, 2003, 2009 by Holman Bible Publishers. Used with permission by Holman Bible Publishers; Nashville, TN. All rights reserved.

Book Pagination & Interior Design—Laura-Lee Booth
Prepared for Publication—Ministry Solutions, LLC

Copyright © 2017 Caleb and Ali Pierce
All rights reserved.

♥♥♥

To our parents, pastors, and mentors:

Thank you for your relentless example of love, purity, and faithfulness. We are forever indebted to you for the deposit you have made in our lives.

CONTENTS

Preface 9

PART I: THE RULES OF DATING

1	Am I ready to start dating?	15
2	What is the best age to start dating?	19
3	Should I wait to date until I think I have found "the one"?	24
4	Does everyone have a soulmate?	27
5	Is it wrong to date behind my parents' back? . . .	32
6	Can a Christian date a non-believer?	36
7	What should I look for in a date?	42
8	Should I be physically attracted to my date? . . .	49
9	What is the appropriate age difference in dating?	54
10	Can I date a guy who's younger than me?	59
11	Is it ok for a girl to ask a guy out?	65
12	Is it ok to date multiple people?	70
13	Can long-distance relationships work?	73
14	Does online dating work?	78

15	What clothes are appropriate to wear to impress someone?	84
16	What are appropriate places to go on dates?	88
17	How can my date and I grow together spiritually?	93
18	How much time is too much time?	98
19	How much should I tell my parents about my relationship?	103
20	I caught my date cheating. Should I take them back?	108
21	What's the best way to break up with someone?	114
22	Can I be friends with my ex?	121
23	How do I handle rumors from a mad ex?	126
24	How should I handle being dumped?	130
25	What's the best way to work out arguments?	134
26	How can I know if my date is controlling?	138
27	Could God be calling me to be single?	145
28	How do I know if I've met the one?	153
29	How do I know if I'm in love?	158
30	How do I know if I'm ready for marriage?	166

PART II: THE RULES OF SEX & PURITY

31	What exactly is sex?	173
32	How far is too far?	177
33	What should I do if I've already gone too far?	181
34	Do you think my date told his friends we went too far?	186
35	Is it ok to date someone who isn't a virgin?	189
36	Should I tell my date about my STD?	193
37	What is safe sex?	198
38	Is oral sex "technically" sex?	202
39	What kind of kissing is appropriate?	208
40	How much PDA is too much?	213
41	Is it a sin to check someone out?	222
42	Is it wrong to have feelings for the same sex?	228
43	How do I break my addiction to porn?	235
44	Is masturbation a sin?	241
45	Do I need to repent for having wet dreams?	245
46	If I know I've found "the one," is sex ok?	249
47	Is it ok to live together before marriage?	252
48	How can my date and I stay sexually pure?	256

49	Do I need an accountability partner?	264
50	Will God really bless my sex life if I wait until marriage to have sex?	268
Conclusion		273

PREFACE

Where do we begin? We started dating as young teenagers. Neither of us even had our license yet. Needless to say, we have experienced some things on this journey. (Ok, not "some" things, actually "a lot" of things—good and bad.)

From the very beginning, we made two major commitments that defined our relationship. First, we made an unwavering decision to keep Christ at the center. Second, we decided that we would stay grounded in the local church. No questions asked, our commitment was continually tested, yet we stayed the course. Consequently, prior to marriage, we dated for six years without ever breaking up and were able to enter marriage as virgins.

Sound too good to be true?

It was the fight of our lives, but by the grace of God and the practical instruction that we are giving you in this book, we made it.

We never intended to write on the subjects of dating, purity, and sex; however, we kept discovering an overwhelming need to discuss issues that the Church, by-and-large, has remained silent on. One day in prayer, loud in our spirits, we heard the Lord say, "If the Church doesn't teach this generation about sexuality, the world will. Whose standard do you want them to follow?"

As we continued to seek God on this matter, it became increasingly clear that our generation needs a revolution in the realm of purity. Our greatest ambition in this life is to see a widespread awakening. No doubt, purity must be one of our chief pursuits in order for this to happen.

When we were growing up, there was never a shortage of people talking about purity and abstinence. There was always someone telling us to keep our virginity and wait until marriage to have sex. Maybe because it had been so long since they had dated, many of them had forgotten that staying pure is much easier said than done. So, even though they told us *what* to avoid, they did not tell us *how* to avoid it.

Sadly, this is still happening.

Consequently, dating has developed a stigma within the Church. Ministers will now publicly and passionately condemn dating altogether, advising this generation to avoid it. There are many problems with this.

The bottom line is this: With or without the Church's consent, this generation is going to date. So, rather than combatting those who want to be in a relationship, we want to help them do it right. It has been our goal in writing this book to give them—you—the practical advice that we so desperately needed while dating.

Many feel hopeless and doomed to fail. Maybe you have already messed up and feel like you are broken beyond repair. It is our hope that as you read through the pages of this book, you will first discover that in Christ you do have what it takes to come out on top. You do not have to follow the path that so many have chosen in this generation.

Secondly, we want you to discover that no matter how far you have gone, with Jesus nothing is ever too far gone. As long as you have a beat in your heart and breath in your lungs, we know that you are not beyond redemption's reach. You can find the power to become, *"... more than conquerors through Him who loved us,"* (Romans 8:37b, NKJV).

Are you ready to begin your journey the right way?

Let's go!

PART I

THE RULES OF DATING

♥♥♥

AM I READY TO START DATING?

We've all heard the age-old saying, "Timing is everything," but is timing everything when it comes to dating? Has God predestined a specific moment where He gives us the green light to date? Ecclesiastes 3:11a (NKJV) says, *"He has made everything beautiful in its time,"* but does this include dating?

Most often, those asking about God's timing are believers whose most earnest desire is to live a life that is pleasing to God. Knowing God's timing on when to date can seem a bit tricky. There is often a fog of confusion surrounding this idea because many have over-spiritualized it.

Can you know if it's God's timing for you to date?

Yes, but you do not have to wait for an audible voice to roar from heaven saying, "I grant you permission to date!"

That's probably *not* going to happen.

Though you should always seek God's will in all things, including dating, don't get tripped up by the search itself. Keep it simple. Start by taking an open, honest evaluation of your personal condition.

Here are three reasons you probably shouldn't date:

1. **You have an inconsistent walk with God.**

    As believers, there is no relationship more important than our relationship with Jesus. There is a belief that if we find "the one," everything will fall into place. That is only a true statement if "the One" you are referring to is God. Until we are successful in our daily devotion to Christ, we will be unsuccessful in every other relationship.

2. **You do not know your self-worth.**

    We've seen more lives damaged than we'd like to admit because they missed this truth. She has low self-esteem; he has deep insecurities—both are broken. Two incomplete people make a complete person, right? Wrong!

    The theory that says, "I'll provide what you are missing, and you'll provide what I'm missing," creates only one thing—a problem! Until you understand how valuable you are to God, you will fight to find your value everywhere else, including a bad relationship.

3. **You are not rooted in a local church.**

    This is a death trap. An old African proverb says, "It takes a village to raise a child." We would dare say it takes a church to raise a healthy relationship.

    The first plague to strike most relationships is the plague of isolation. You're head-over-heels in love. (You know what we're talking about.) Everything else in the world fades away, and it's just you and them.

    And that's where it all starts to go wrong.

    It's true, we were designed to have only one significant other, but we were not designed to have only one relationship. We believe the secret key to healthy dating is being rooted in the local church. If you are not rooted in a community of believers, dating should not even be considered. If you want to find someone who will be faithful to you, look for someone who is faithful to the house of God.

If you are looking to know if it is God's timing for you to date, evaluating your life in these three areas will point you in the right direction. If you are inconsistent in your daily devotion, have no understanding of your value in Christ, and are not rooted in a local church, then you should not consider dating.

But once these areas are in order, the coast is clear. Get your date on!

2

WHAT IS THE BEST AGE TO START DATING?

Can you remember your first real crush? Of course you can! Most likely, you saw them running across the playground and something sparked inside you. It was at that moment it all began.

So what, did you marry your second grade sweetheart?

Probably not.

Why did you even fall for them in the first place?

Attraction starts young. Most kids experience their first crush in elementary school. It's just the way we were made.

So, how should we handle it? Should we work to suppress our desires until we hit some magical age? We can say from experience that only makes it worse!

To determine what the appropriate age is for dating, you've got to define "dating." In our culture, we have different ideas surrounding this concept. Rather than giving you an age, we're going to define three stages of dating. Read each description to determine what stage of dating best fits the phase of life you're in.

STAGE ONE: DATING TO DEVELOP

This is the super flirty stage. This is where you're intrigued by the person of interest, but marriage isn't a realistic option. Do your palms still get sweaty every time they walk in the room? If yes, then you're probably in this stage.

One of the key highlights of this phase might be that you can finally update your social profile status from "Single" to "In a Relationship."

This stage won't last forever for one of two reasons: Either the relationship will just end, or it will progress further into Stage Two. Regardless of the longevity of this stage, it is still valuable. During this time, make the most of learning the do's and don'ts of dating. The greatest benefit you'll get at this point in the game is personal development which is vital to your future relational success.

Here, you learn dating etiquette. For example, men (hopefully) learn to be gentlemen and open the door for the ladies. (And, ladies, learn to appreciate his efforts here.) In this stage, it's important to take mental notes of your mistakes, so you don't carry them into the next phase.

The "Dating to Develop" stage is the starting point for all relationships but is most prominent among those in their teens and early twenties.

STAGE TWO: DATING TO DISCOVER

Here's where you're testing the waters. At this stage, you allow the relationship to progress to the point that your date's imperfections start to surface. They slowly stop trying to keep their act together every time you come around. Consequently, you will discover a lot more of their true character.

In this part of the process, you'll be able to determine with greater clarity than ever before what you're really looking for and what you're really looking to avoid in a relationship.

At this phase, dating the wrong person can actually be very valuable.

Now, hold on! We're not at all suggesting that you intentionally go find someone you shouldn't date and hook up with them. However, chances are this will happen to you at some point. Maybe you're already in a relationship you know isn't going to last. Since you're going to break up, does that mean you've just wasted your time?

No, of course not. You have two choices: You can either give up on dating altogether, or you can choose to grow from your experience. Since you will most likely end up dating someone other than "the one," learn from it!

Ask yourself:

- *What was it about them that I couldn't get past?*

- *Is our relationship ending because they have certain personality traits that I'm not compatible with?*

Ask these questions, so you can avoid getting into another relationship with someone who has the same problems. Use this time to discover what you do and do not want to live with for the rest of your life.

Many begin this phase right out of high school, entering America's mating grounds, a.k.a. college.

STAGE THREE: DATING TO DECIDE

"Dating to Decide" is the bridge between "Dating to Discover" and engagement. There's an old word which actually defines this stage. It's one that we, as a generation, have unfortunately lost. That word is "courting."

To "court," simply means to date with the intention of marriage. At this stage of the process, you've got a hunch that who you're with is who you'll marry. Realistically, this phase is only for those who can handle the logistics of marriage.

Here are a few questions you can ask yourself to determine if you are ready for the "Dating to Decide" stage:

- *Can I hold a job?*

- *Do I pay my bills on time?*

- *As a couple, would we have the resources to support our household?*

At this phase, under the guidance of a trusted mentor (specifically, a pastor), if your relationship is in good health and can be sustained financially, wedding bells could be just around the corner. (If you are still in middle or high school, sorry to burst your bubble; this phase isn't applicable to you yet! You need to be of legal age.)

Regardless what stage you are in, keep your priorities straight. It makes no difference whether you're going on your very first date ever or you're about to say, "I do." The ultimate secret to a successful relationship is keeping Jesus in the center of all you do.

3

SHOULD I WAIT TO DATE UNTIL I THINK I HAVE FOUND "THE ONE"?

While there are exceptions to nearly every rule, for the most part, we believe it's safe to say that you cannot find "the one" without actually searching for them.

One of the first clues to finding the person God has called you to be with is often realized by discovering who He has not called you to be with.

The plan of heaven for your life is typically hidden just far enough beneath the surface that God requires you to dig a little before you can find it.

King Solomon's words, recorded in Proverbs 25:2 (NKJV), are certainly applicable in this matter. He said, *"It is the glory of God to conceal a matter, but the glory of kings is to search out a matter."*

If you wait until you find "the one" to start dating, you might not ever get to start. You've got to change your focus.

Rather than looking for "the one" from the get-go, look to navigate your dating life in a way that honors Christ.

Here are two principles to follow in your pursuit of dating in a way that's pleasing to God:

1. **Search under the guidance of the Holy Spirit.**

    In Galatians 5:16 (NKJV), Paul wrote under divine inspiration, *". . . Walk in the Spirit, and you shall not fulfill the lust of the flesh."* This is the most important principle to follow.

    If you do not follow the leading of the Spirit, you are certain to follow the leading of your carnal appetite—and in the world of dating, that never ends well. You'll settle for someone who looks good in their twenties but still can't provide in their forties.

    The Holy Spirit is the perfect matchmaker, and He wants to help you in this critical pursuit. So, ask Him to help. Tell Him what you want, ask Him what He wants, and listen to what He says. Once He speaks, write it down, and you're almost ready to start the hunt.

2. **Search under the guidance of a trusted mentor.**

    In the realm of romance, with raging desires, we can easily mistake our wishes for the voice of the Lord. This is where we need some trusted advisors.

When your emotions are high, typically, your discernment is low. The line between right and wrong seems to be a little vague. Emotions can be very deceptive! Now, listen. We are not saying dating should be lifeless and boring. No way! It's meant to be vibrant and exciting. However, you must be intentional about making decisions with a sober mind. It's highly unlikely that you'll be able to do this when Mr. or Miss Perfect shows some interest in you.

This is why the voice of someone who you know wants the best for you is so crucial. We should never make any major life decisions alone. We should always make these decisions under the guidance of people who are further down the road than we are. The best place to find someone like this is in the Church.

Seek guidance, seek wisdom, and be intentional about finding your mate under Godly supervision.

If you're already in a relationship, it's not too late to make these changes. If you will choose to pursue God's plan for your life and your relationships today, it could keep you from unnecessary wounds tomorrow.

DOES EVERYONE HAVE A SOULMATE?

Are you looking for "the one?"—you know, your "other half"? The idea of having a "soulmate" stems from Greek mythology. Plato, the ancient Greek philosopher, is credited for having taught that humans were originally both male and female in one body having four arms, four legs, and two faces on their head.

What a picture!

The story is that the Greek god, Zeus, separated them, thus placing humans on a conquest to find their other half.

This theory, however, does not coincide with the Bible. While scripture is clear that upon marriage, husband and wife become one flesh, this does not mean—nor is there any biblical evidence—that they were incomplete souls searching for their other half prior to that.

Two incomplete people do not make a complete person.

So, does this mean that God did not create a soulmate for you? Does every "Adam" have an "Eve"? We'll leave that for you to decide. But when making your decision, there are three things you need to consider:

1. **There is a plan.**

   > *"The steps of a good man are ordered by the Lord...,"*
   >
   > Psalms 37:23a (NKJV)

   Have you ever heard the phrase: "Hindsight is twenty-twenty"? It's certainly been true for us. The more we grow, the more we are able to recognize that God has been working His plan in our lives all along, even during our dating years.

   As a follower of Christ, your life is not your own. This doesn't mean that God is forcing you to abide in His plan, but He is directing your path more than you realize—and that is good news!

   You don't have to walk around on eggshells, afraid that you might date the wrong person and ultimately destroy God's plan for your life and marriage. Before we started dating, we had been in other relationships and survived. God's plan for your life is not that fragile. This doesn't mean that you should carelessly date just anyone.

But the truth is, though you are ultimately responsible for your life, you can rest knowing that God has your steps ordered.

Keep your confidence.

If marriage is part of the plan, as long as you follow His lead, you'll get the right person.

2. There is a preference.

> *"To the unmarried and the widows I say that it is good for them to remain single, as I am."*
>
> 1 Corinthians 7:8 (ESV)

Don't freak out! This isn't a "Thou shalt . . ." command; it's just a preference. Check it out. The next verse proves it: (9a) *"But if they cannot exercise self-control, they should marry."*

While this may not be a command, it does convey an interesting point. The apostle Paul, the most prominent and arguably the most important person in the New Testament, outside of Jesus, preferred that believers remain unmarried.

We are not advocating celibacy. We are, however, wanting to affirm a great truth: Being single does not mean that you are incomplete. You do not have to find "the one" you are "meant to be with" *before* you walk in wholeness.

What does this mean?

If God is in the business of preselecting a spouse for those who are destined for marriage, fine. If He isn't, guess what? That's fine, too!

The point is that you do not have to have a relationship to be complete.

3. **There is a pursuit.**

> *"He who finds a wife finds a good thing..."*
> Proverbs 18:22a (NKJV)

This is the life-verse for 90% of all Christian bachelors! Anyone single and ready to mingle?

So far in this chapter, we've discovered that God has a plan and the Bible has a preference. Now we come to the final point: You have a pursuit.

If you are looking to marry one day, you'll eventually have to start pursuing a mate. You'll either pursue a life of independence as a single person or start searching for a potential spouse.

This verse makes your future love life a bit complicated. It puts the ball on your side of the court, making *you* responsible for finding a mate.

Regardless of whether or not God performs "divine setups," those who make up the singles' community must be intentional about finding that "good thing" the Lord has predestined for them. If you want to end up with a spouse, then you have a part to play in the grand scheme of love and marriage. One thing is for sure: If you don't find them, you won't get them.

What camp do you identify with? Do you believe that there is just one particular person called to be your mate? Or, do you believe that it's ultimately up to you to find a compatible companion?

Regardless where you stand, you can rest in this great truth: If you will delight yourself in the Lord, then He will give you the desires of your heart. (See Psalms 37:4.) You can trust the Lord with your future.

Here are our final words of instruction. While you should not be casual about who you date, neither should you carry an unbearable burden. Pray first and approach it seriously but not fearfully. Be sober, yet don't be timid. You're not going to ruin God's plan for your life. If you will simply seek the Lord in all you do, you will find the exact person who's most suitable for you.

5

IS IT WRONG TO DATE BEHIND MY PARENTS' BACK?

There are a myriad of different approaches parents take with their kids dating. Some restrict them from all dating; others have a stringent refining process.

Whatever the method may or may not be, one thing is for sure: Sometimes parents and kids do not see eye-to-eye. This can make for some tense moments of extreme turmoil.

What do you do if there is someone you really like, but your parents aren't giving you the "green light" to date?

Here's the real question: What would you do if you could do it without them ever really knowing?

We want to challenge you. As a Christian, the answer should be quite obvious. There are three primary reasons you do not want to date behind your parents' back:

1. **It's not biblical.**

   "'Honor your father and mother.'"

   Ephesians 6:2a (NLT)

   If you are a Christian, since this is in the Bible, you really do not have much of an option. Oh, sure, you could rebel against God's Word if you want, but you certainly won't have His blessing on your relationship. As believers, even when our opinions and preferences differ, we must choose to subject our lives to the principles and commands found in scripture above all else.

   There will be times, no doubt, that this will frustrate your plans. However, amidst your frustration, if you will choose to honor your parents and their wishes, God will honor you—and without His blessing, no relationship can succeed.

2. **They are smarter than you.**

   "Listen, my sons, to a father's instruction; pay attention and gain understanding."

   Proverbs 4:1 (NIV)

   This might be hard to believe. We promise we aren't lying. Your parents—they actually know more than you do.

   Shocking, isn't it?

They've been telling you for years, but it's actually the truth. They have been around the block a few times. Their life experiences give them something you need—wisdom!

Believe it or not, they really aren't trying to ruin your life when they tell you they don't want you dating a certain individual. They are actually trying to protect you. While you are all caught up in the moment, blinded by what you see, they aren't. Their lack of enthusiasm, as annoying as it may be at times, is actually a safe guard.

If you find someone who can pass this test and your parents give you the thumbs up, you may have found someone who's worth the investment. In the meantime, trust your parents. You need their wisdom!

3. You will reap what you sow.

> *"My experience shows that those who plant trouble and cultivate evil will harvest the same."*
>
> Job 4:8 (NLT)

Have you ever heard the old phrase, "The apple doesn't fall far from the tree?" Though you are the apple right now, one day you will probably be the tree. You are going to be that annoying parent who doesn't like their child's dating preferences. It may be hard to imagine at this stage of life, but try to think about how you, as a parent, would want your kid to respond to you.

Guess what?

That's how you need to respond to your parents. It's not just some old cliché. You really will reap in your children what you have sown. If you are whiney and bratty every time your parents tell you something you don't want to hear, get ready because one day it's going to come right back at you.

If you implement these three phases now, they will save you from a lot of trouble. At this stage of life, everything seems so dramatic. But we promise you, even when your parents' instructions make you feel as though the world is going to end, everything is going to be alright. You will make it through it just fine.

As a matter of fact, one day you will probably look back and actually say, "Thank you!" If you could see things for what they really are, your parents and those who God has placed over you at this stage of life are really some of your greatest assets. Take heed to their instructions. They really do have your best interests at heart.

6

CAN A CHRISTIAN DATE A NON-BELIEVER?

Is it really that risky to date someone who doesn't share the same beliefs as you? The apostle Paul wrote, *"Don't team up with those who are unbelievers. How can righteousness be a partner with wickedness? How can light live with darkness?"* (2 Corinthians 6:14, NLT)

Sadly, we've watched many choose to date a non-believer at the expense of their walk with Christ. You may be able to have a successful relationship, according to the world's standard, but you cannot date a non-believer and have a successful relationship according to God's standard.

For believers, there are three different types of people that fall into the category of being "unequally yoked":

(1.) Those of other religions.

(2.) Those of no religion.

(3.) Those with stark religious differences.

Being in a dating relationship with any of these three types of people will inevitably lead to major problems. For example, it would be very difficult for a Protestant and a Catholic to have a strong relationship. The differences in their beliefs are vast and could ultimately cause great tension, especially if marriage is in your future.

Being unequally yoked with someone in dating will lead to negative side-effects in these three areas of your life:

1. **Sexually.**

> *"'Therefore, come out from among unbelievers, and separate yourselves from them, says the Lord.'"*
>
> 2 Corinthians 6:17 (NLT)

Paul actually wrote this to a church that was steeped in sexual promiscuity. Maybe he knew that part of the solution in defeating this particular sin was to separate from those who saw nothing wrong with it.

When you surround yourself with people who live by a different standard of morals, your convictions will be put to the test every time. You can't expect sinners to live like saints. For a non-believer, choosing to abstain from sex until marriage doesn't make any sense. This often results in them pressuring the person of faith to compromise their beliefs. So, if you choose to oppose Scripture and date someone who is not following Christ, you may very well find yourself in the heat of such pressure.

Here's our advice: Don't play with fire. Your sexual purity is too valuable.

2. Spiritually.

> *"As Solomon grew old, his wives turned his heart after other gods, and his heart was not fully devoted to the Lord his God, as the heart of David his father had been."*
>
> 1 Kings 11:4 (NIV)

The law of gravity teaches us that it is easier for something to fall than it is for something to rise. This is the primary reason we do not condone Christians dating those outside of the faith. We do not believe in "missionary dating." You know, the idea of "flirt to convert."

Yeah, that doesn't work.

It is, however, very tempting to buy into the idea that you are above "falling away" when you find someone you are really attracted to that does not have a relationship with Christ. Have you ever thought, "I could change them," or, "I will win them to the Lord"? So did we. But the truth is even ol' Solomon, the wisest man to ever live, couldn't escape gravity. He fell into this very trap and began worshipping other gods. If you choose to date someone outside of the faith, you may be shocked to look back one day and discover the person you thought you would change has changed you.

3. **Socially.**

> *"Only let your manner of life be worthy of the gospel of Christ, so that whether I come and see you or am absent, I may hear of you that you are standing firm in one spirit, with one mind striving side by side for the faith of the gospel..."*
>
> Philippians 1:27 (ESV)

If we were to randomly ask your classmates or colleagues to tell us in one sentence who you are, what would they say? What opinion do others have about you? Would they immediately think of your walk with Christ?

Your social reputation is more important than you may realize. There is a lot that goes into the way someone forms an opinion about who you are. However, one of the key ingredients people use when forming an opinion about someone is who they are associated with. If you are one with the world, you cannot be one with Christ.

There are really only two options: You can either confront the culture or conform to it, but you cannot do both. When you choose to date someone whose lifestyle is contrary to Christianity, you do so at the expense of your influence. This is a devastating blow to your reputation.

Our society does not notice those who blend in. If you want to make an impact, you must stand out. When people see that you are dating someone who is either a non-believer or a weak Christian, they will inevitably put you in the same category as them.

If you want to remain strong sexually, spiritually, and socially, then who you choose to date can be no small matter of choice. It is sadly becoming more and more common for followers of Christ to date those outside of the faith. As you can see, those who do so are walking into a trap.

We do not believe that all non-believers are bad, but they are headed in a different direction. To form a relationship would mean that someone has to compromise. It's not only dangerous, as we've stated, to date someone outside of the faith, but you are also taking a huge risk when you date anyone who is weak in their relationship with Jesus. If you have been following Christ for five years, it's probably not a good idea to date someone who's just been following Him for five minutes.

We challenge you, as a believer, to make a quality commitment to avoid dating anyone who is not on the same spiritual trajectory. In the end, you will be glad you did.

7

WHAT SHOULD I LOOK FOR IN A DATE?

Finding a date is easy. Finding a good date . . . Well, that's a different story.

As believers, we should never approach this kind of relationship flippantly. Whatever we invest in we are influenced by. If you are going to make the time, energy, and emotional investment into a relationship, it should be with someone worthwhile.

When you've found an individual you like, link up with a trusted mentor or your local pastor and ask for their advice. There is no "one size fits all" when it comes to what you should look for in dating. That's why you need leaders in your life who can help you make wise decisions.

However, there are seven non-negotiables that everyone should look for when it comes to dating:

1. **Someone who has made God their first priority.**

   > *"'You shall love the Lord your God with all your heart, with all your soul, with all your strength, and with all your mind,' and 'your neighbor as yourself.'"*
   >
   > Luke 10:27 (NKJV)

   We firmly believe that you cannot love your neighbor as yourself until you love God with all of your being. This means that until the person you are crushing on loves Jesus more than anything else, they cannot love you the way you deserve to be loved. This may seem a little old school, but there is still no better place to find your date than in the house of God. Who do you know who's faithful in the local church? Are they single, ready to mingle? Stay on the lookout!

2. **Someone of a good reputation.**

   > *"A good name is to be chosen rather than great riches, loving favor rather than silver and gold."*
   >
   > Proverbs 22:1 (NKJV)

   Everyone, to some degree, is known for something. Maybe it's their boldness, their bashful personality, or in some cases, a bad past.

Have you ever heard the saying "Love is blind?" Sadly, this old adage has proven true time and time again. While we do not believe in holding someone's past against them, when they've surrendered their life to Jesus, neither do we believe in ignoring bad character traits and actions just because we "like" them.

Unless someone has committed their life to following Christ, you can tell a lot about where they are going based upon where they've been. If they've got a bad past behind them, then don't go into their bad future with them.

3. **Someone with good friendships.**

> *"'bad company corrupts good character.'"*
> 1 Corinthians 15:33b (NLT)

Jim Rohn's famous statement, "We are the average of the five people we spend the most time with," is an essential guide when determining who could make a great date. Look for someone who hangs around people of great character. Without becoming a stalker, see who they are associated with and who makes up their inner circle. The more you discover about those they are involved with, the more you ultimately discover about them.

4. **Someone who models a life of consistency and stability.**

   > *"Oh that my ways may be steadfast in keeping your statutes!"*
   >
   > Psalms 119:5 (ESV)

   You do not want to get involved in a relationship with someone who changes their life's direction every time the wind blows. Look for someone who is consistent in their daily walk with God and is establishing a lifestyle that can be built upon.

   This becomes increasingly more important as you reach the age where dating could lead to marriage. Listen, you really don't want to get stuck with someone you are having to cater to. Playing the role of a parent in a dating relationship is just weird. Consistency and stability are key components in every strong relationship.

5. **Someone who exemplifies a life of hospitality.**

   > *"Be hospitable to one another without grumbling."*
   >
   > 1 Peter 4:9 (NKJV)

   You don't want to date anyone who is so self-absorbed that they never think of putting the desires of others before their own. Otherwise, you'll end up in a relationship with someone who treats you as if you are their servant.

The best way we've learned to detect whether or not someone is truly hospitable is by getting them around those who cannot benefit them. How do they act with young children or the elderly? What about someone with special needs? Are they kind to them?

You want someone who demonstrates genuine hospitality from the heart, not one who acts only to impress.

Ladies, this is especially true when looking for a guy. For example, if you go on a first date with a guy who doesn't pay for your meal, make sure that's the last date you go on with them. If he doesn't show hospitality at first, he won't later either. Move on.

6. Someone you are physically attracted to.

> *"How beautiful you are, my darling, how beautiful!"*
>
> Song of Songs 1:15a (NLT)

If you've spent any time reading Song of Solomon (or, as the *New Living Translation* calls it, Song of Songs), you know one thing's for sure: These two were really attracted to each other. Physical appearance is not everything, but it is still very important.

We're not saying you shouldn't date someone unless they've won a beauty pageant, but we do want you to know that it is not superficial to decide that you are not interested in someone because of their looks. If they have an excellent personality, but you gag every time you see them, they're probably not what God has in mind for you. Physical attraction does matter!

7. Someone you could build a friendship with.

> *"A friend loves at all times . . ."*
>
> Proverbs 17:17a (NKJV)

The best relationships are not built on looks or romance; they're built on friendship. I'm sure you've seen the cartoon of the girl praying that reads: "God, give me a man, someone I can fall in love with!" Then it shows an image portraying God that says, "I did, and you keep calling him your best friend."

This is huge!

When you share life with someone, at some point, they are going to see some of your flaws.

If they are around you long enough, they'll realize that their knight in shining armor has a few dings from battle. That's why you cannot afford to build your relationship around superficial qualities.

When looking for a date, you need to ask yourself:

- *Do our personalities mesh well?*
- *Do we share any common interests?*
- *Do I find their company enjoyable?*

To determine whether or not you should invest in a relationship, these questions can help eliminate empty opportunities with people who would ultimately waste your time. This may require going on a couple of dates, so you can learn more about them. Once you've done that, if the only thing you like about them is their looks, pull the plug.

Stay on the lookout! If you find someone who matches these seven qualities, you've found a potential candidate. While this process may make things a little bit more tedious, remember: You are far too valuable to invest yourself into just any given relationship.

Be patient, stay hopeful, and trust that God knows the desires of your heart!

8

SHOULD I BE PHYSICALLY ATTRACTED TO MY DATE?

We love to ask couples what it was about their spouse that first sparked their interest. In response, we've heard many different answers. Yet, the most common trait they first noticed was their looks.

A successful relationship consists of many different components. However, most often, it all starts with what someone sees. How important is someone's appearance? Do you need to revamp the way you project yourself to attract a new date?

Here are three things you must know about looks:

1. Looks are important.

> *"You are altogether beautiful, my darling, beautiful in every way."*
>
> Song of Songs 4:7 (NLT)

Clearly, Solomon, who wrote this, thought looks were important! (By the way, he was the wisest man to ever live.) On numerous occasions, we have heard people who were desperate for love say, "Oh, it's not about the looks." After they've told us various traits they were looking for in a mate, they are typically shocked when we respond, "Oh, that's great . . . but what about their appearance?"

Somewhere along the way, especially among Christians, the importance of physical attraction has developed a bit of a stigma. People have bought into the idea that they are being selfish or shallow if they lack interest in an individual because of their looks.

This is absurd!

It's neither noble nor godly to date someone you find unattractive. If your relationship progresses to marriage, you had better hope you find them attractive on your wedding night, or you will kill the romance!

Bottom line, do not date someone you do not find attractive!

2. Looks are not everything.

> "What matters is not your outer appearance—the styling of your hair, the jewelry

you wear, the cut of your clothes—but your inner disposition."

1 Peter 3:3 (MSG)

We're not trying to confuse you. We meant what you read a minute ago. Looks really are important, but here's the catch: They're not everything.

You have heard the old idiom: "There's more than meets the eye." Is this true with the person you are interested in?

There are a few things that commonly happen when it comes to dating and physical attraction:

(1.) You find someone who looks stunning, but they have a sorry attitude.

(2.) You find someone with a phenomenal personality, but you can't find a single thing about their physical appearance that you find attractive.

(3.) You get the dream package—good looks *and* a good personality.

Then, there's one more.

(4.) The person who has a stellar personality with physical features you could learn to like—and, by the way, this happens a lot.

Do not shut someone down because they don't look like they just walked off a fashion runway. If their appearance is something you could learn to like, embrace them for that which is beyond what initially meets the eye.

3. **Looks will fade.**

> *"Charm is deceptive, and beauty is fleeting; but a woman who fears the Lord is to be praised."*
>
> Proverbs 31:30 (NIV)

It comes for us all. At some point, you will wake up, look in the mirror and think, "How did this happen?" Gray hair, sagging skin, and wrinkles—even the best have to face it.

The truth is, that beautiful woman you are chasing after right now will not look like that forever. If the basis of your relationship with someone is their looks, you are headed for disaster. Inevitably, your foundation will begin falling apart when their enticing appearance begins to fade.

When it comes to physical attraction, never let it become the foundation of your relationship.

There is far more to discover and find appealing. When natural beauty has been swallowed up by age, chances are their humor, wisdom, and compassion will be more vibrant than ever before.

We want to wrap this up by encouraging you. If you, like so many of us, battle insecurities with your physical appearance, know that you really are *"fearfully and wonderfully made."* (See Psalms 139:14.) Should you put effort into the way you look? If you want to find a good date, then, yes. But, don't get wrapped up in trying to attract someone. You are not defined by the opinion someone else has about your appearance.

The only thing that can truly define you is the opinion that God has about you, and He thought you were worth giving His life for. In the eyes of your King, you are treasured!

9

WHAT IS THE APPROPRIATE AGE DIFFERENCE IN DATING?

Want to know what the Bible says about this question?

It doesn't.

We're given a couple of implications and examples, but that's about it. Both Proverbs 5:18 and Malachi 2:14 reference *"the wife of your youth,"* which could imply that both the man and the woman were still in a youthful state; but this alone is speculation.

Genesis 17:17 (NKJV) records Abram saying, *"Shall a child be born to a man who is one hundred years old? And shall Sarah, who is ninety years old, bear a child?"* From this we know there was a ten-year age gap between ol' Abe and his lady. Should this one example be our standard?

While the Bible doesn't give chapter and verse clarity on the subject, there are various factors we should take into consideration when it comes to the appropriate age gap in dating.

Here are three key factors to take into consideration:

1. **It must be legal.**

    As you get older, a moderate age gap becomes less of an issue. However, when a minor is involved, things are much more complicated. If you are over the age of 18 and are dating someone under the age of 18, then your relationship is a legal matter; and sexual conduct is a legal violation with hefty, life-altering consequences.

    Someone reading this is probably thinking, "Well, we're not having sex, so what's the big deal?" Here's the big deal: You're love drunk. With a tainted perception, you're most likely convinced that your relationship will last forever. But as outsiders, talking soberly, we need you to know that a bad break-up—which is probable—could put you behind bars. It is not just intercourse that leads to trouble.

    Your late nights of touchy, feely romance can be interpreted much differently by a livid ex. Just one accusation has the potential of leaving you branded as a sex offender for the rest of your life.

    Can you date a minor without it being a problem? Yes, but it's risky. With parental consent, we did it, and here's how:

When we were 17 and 19, we were very intentional about keeping everything public. Our dates were primarily church and family outings. We chose not to trust ourselves. Privacy will only jeopardize purity, so we avoided it like a plague. Did we want to? No, but looking back, we're so glad we did.

Here's the take away: If you're in that awkward spot where a minor is involved, keep everything public. Otherwise, avoid dating a minor at all costs. If you're out of your teen years, leave minors alone. You can find someone else or wait until they're legal. If they're "the one," then they're worth the wait.

2. **Maturity.**

While you don't want to feel like you are babysitting your date, neither do you want to feel like you're going out with your parent or someone who's on a totally different playing field. That's just weird.

There should be a fairly mutual maturity level shared within the relationship to avoid facing these problems. Where there is a larger age gap, you will typically find greater distance between maturity levels. There are certain hurdles this creates that can be almost insurmountable. For example, women have an amazing gift that really starts to show up in their late teens and early twenties. This gift is their maternal instinct. While this instinct is awesome when it comes to children, it's totally different when it comes to men.

Ladies, he's not looking for you to be his momma. But, if in the relationship, the guy is younger than the girl, the woman may find this instinct heightened simply because of the maturity gap.

The tension between ages is not as big of an issue when the guy is older than the girl. While there is nothing wrong with it, there tends to be more of a hurdle to cross when the girl is older than the guy. Ultimately, this is something you can get past as long as there isn't a great chasm between maturity levels. With age, this issue tends to fade.

3. The circle of life.

You've got to think ahead. This is especially true if you are at an age that allows you the liberty to pursue marriage should the relationship progress. If you are in your early twenties and end up marrying someone in their mid-to-late thirties, there are some real liabilities you're nearly certain to face in the future.

Two people come to mind when we think of couples who had a successful marriage even though they married someone significantly older than them later in life. Both of these women will recount their years of marriage as the most joyful years of their life, but today both of these women are widows and still have a lot of life ahead of them.

When you pursue a relationship with a significant age gap, you've got to be prepared to face things in the end that seem irrelevant in the beginning. Retirement, health, and even death are realities that are nearly certain to ensue.

You cross different phases of life at totally different times, and this could present some real challenges in a marriage. While you technically can marry someone who is significantly older or younger, we don't recommend it. The stories of those who have successfully taken this approach are few and far between. We find it best to approach it as the exception to the rule.

When it comes to love, is age just a number? No, it matters! To build a long-lasting, healthy relationship, we challenge you to take the keys we've mentioned here and implement them as you move forward on your journey!

10

CAN I DATE A GUY WHO'S YOUNGER THAN ME?

While the Bible has a lot to say about relationships, it does not present any age restrictions as to whether or not a lady can date a man younger than her. The Bible does, however, tell us that God has appointed authority to rule in the land. So, if you are over the age of 18 and are trying to hook up with a minor, you are not only defying the laws that have been established by our government; you are also defying the instruction of God.

But what about a lady in her late twenties dating someone in their early twenties? Do you identify with this?

We've got good news. It can work! But, as it is with any relationship, this type of dating scenario doesn't come without obstacles.

Ladies, we have three questions you need to ask yourselves. Men, we didn't leave you out. There are also three questions you men have to ask yourselves.

We were always taught that ladies go first, so we will start with them:

LADIES, CAN YOU HANDLE...

1. **Being led and protected by a man who is younger than you?**

    We once watched a comical movie where a mom and her son were awakened by the sound of what they thought was an intruder. Before finding out that the noise came from a shelf in their kitchen breaking, they both jumped out of bed. The boy ran for his toy gun and said, "Get behind me, Momma! I'll protect you!" to which the mother chuckled and replied, "No, you better let me take this one."

    If you catch yourself chuckling, as this mother did, when you think of being led and protected by the younger guy you are interested in, then you need to move on. The thought of his protection shouldn't make you laugh; it should make you feel secure.

2. **The maturity gap?**

    Age doesn't always equal maturity. However, the longer you are alive, the more experience you tend to have—and maturity almost always comes as a result of experience.

We learn from life's adventures.

Ladies, if you are dating someone who's five years younger than you, there may be some crucial things that you have been through that they haven't. This could mean they are not yet developed in areas that you are.

Can you handle having aspects of life where you are on different pages? If not, the maturity factor could cripple the relationship.

3. Feeling out of place?

There is a strong chance that the circle of friends the man you are interested in consists of people all around the same age as him. If they all want to hang out, you may find yourself feeling a little out of place.

If you are like most people, meeting strangers can already be awkward enough. Over time, after hanging around his sphere of friends, the awkwardness should subside. But, is this something you can handle in the meantime?

If not, it could be another sign that you need to move on.

MEN, DO YOU HAVE THE CONFIDENCE NEEDED TO . . .

1. **Lead and protect a lady who is older than you?**

   Any man who tells you he has never battled with insecurities is lying. All men have. Yet, dating a woman who's older than you could heighten those insecurities. Initially, if you find yourself struggling with this, don't sweat it. Feelings of inadequacy may try to pop up in the beginning of your relationship. However, if you find yourself continuing to struggle with it after a few months, you may need to move on.

   Do you have the courage to overcome this and offer your lady the leadership and protection she deserves? If not, this doesn't make you weak; it simply means you aren't the right fit for this kind of relationship. Move on!

2. **Stand in the midst of opposition?**

   No doubt, you'll hear from the naysayers. You will be amazed at the people who purposefully go out of their way to give you their opinion. This is most difficult when it comes from those closest to you.

   Can you handle bearing the brunt of others' jokes? If you are easily triggered by someone else's negative opinions, this may be your greatest challenge in having a date who's older than you.

The connection you share with her could be phenomenal. Yet, with the amount of criticism this kind of relationship could potentially attract, especially from friends, you may find it unbearable and disorienting. You will either have to learn how to move past what others think about you or pull the plug on dating ladies who are older than you.

3. **Embrace the stage of life they are in?**

We have good friends who have had to learn this principle first-hand. He is 21; she is 24. While he is still working on getting his degree, she is already out of college and is a full-time teacher.

While it may take some time, learning to embrace and celebrate the different stage of life that your lady is in, is a crucial component to a healthy relationship. You cannot afford to be jealous or envious that she is ahead of you. If you are going to foster an atmosphere that allows your relationship to grow, she has to know you are excited about her achievements and that you support her wholeheartedly.

In closing, we want to encourage you. Don't jump into a relationship too hastily. First, spend time in prayer. This is an emotional decision, which can make hearing from God a little difficult. When you are facing a situation, like this one, where you could easily mistake your preference for God's will, do yourself one final favor and seek the advice of someone you can trust, preferably a trusted spiritual leader. What does your pastor think of the situation?

Are you considering someone who's really too young? Once you have asked yourself these questions—and answered them—you will know more clearly if dating someone with an age gap is for you or not.

IS IT OK FOR A GIRL TO ASK A GUY OUT?

It seems as though our society is abandoning anything and everything that deals with moral excellence. While some things in age's past, were simply a matter of preference, other things were strong, healthy practices that every society would benefit from should they adhere to them.

One of these things is the practice of chivalry. Since our generation has neglected this practice, our guess is that some of you may not even know what chivalry means. So, check it out. By definition, to be chivalrous is:

"to behave in an honorable and polite way, especially toward women."[1]

In a society where it is becoming more and more socially acceptable for a lady to take the initiative, we want to cut

---

1 http://www.learnersdictionary.com/definition/chilvrous.

against the grain. We believe this question has far more to do with the condition of our culture than it does with dating.

The restoration of chivalry among men is imperative. So, ladies, we've got a couple of questions you should consider when contemplating whether or not you should ask him out:

1. **If I have to chase him, is he really worth my time?**

    We know there are exceptions to the rule, but we believe that it should not be the norm for ladies to do the chasing.

    Let me ask, do you tend to take better care of what has been given to you or what you have purchased? I can still remember when my parents gave me my first cell phone. I took such good care of that thing . . . for a few weeks, at least. Then, I steadily became more and more causal with it, eventually breaking it because of my carelessness.

    Fast forward a couple of years. I got a job, and my phone and phone bill were then my responsibility. Guess how I handled *that* phone when I was the one making the payments? With care and protection? You bet!

While you are not a product that's up for sale, you are a woman who is worth the energy and effort a good man will put forth to get you. Our first piece of advice is that you refrain from chasing him; let him run after you. A man who will not chase you before marriage will never chase you after marriage.

Think about it. When you consider the longevity of relationships from the past, you can clearly see that we are missing something they had: Marriages lasted and families were strong. Sadly, that has become a rare find in our day.

This demands that we stop to consider the missing link. Could it be that relationships were stronger in the past because men were expected to take the initiative? To regain quality relationships, we must once again embrace the principles of chivalry. If you want to build something that's going to last, history proves that it is most effective when he makes the first move.

2. Am I playing too hard to get?

When I was looking to find Ali's engagement ring, I must have driven the jeweler crazy. I am certain I asked to see at least a thousand rings. To be quite honest, I even thought to myself, "They could avoid me asking to see a different ring every thirty seconds if they'd just put them outside of the glass." I know I must have been annoying them.

Why do they keep those rings locked up behind the glass counters anyway? Because things of great value aren't easily accessible.

Ladies, you don't need to be within everybody's reach.

Now, with that being said, there is another revelation you must get. You know how those guys who flirt with you tend to act like they've got it all together? Most of that is a cover up. He acts cool in front of you, but you really intimidate him. While you should "play hard to get," you shouldn't make it impossible for him. You've already got him wiping sweat from his brow every time you turn around.

When someone asks to see a ring at the jewelry store, they do not ignore them simply to make them ask a few more times. That would just be wrong.

When you notice that a guy you like is inquiring to know more about you, don't keep hiding. Ultimately, that ring wasn't made to be behind glass; it was made to be on a hand. Give him hints and drop some signals. Now, just a side note: You'll have to be patient while he catches on. Guys speak a totally different language than girls. If you are really interested in him, as an act of courtesy, find subtle ways to let him know that you're not going to humiliate him if he pursues you.

We know these principles make guys a little nervous. Why? Because it raises the bar. Quite frankly, we don't need any more men running around who devalue women.

Ladies, you deserve the best! You deserve a guy who will pursue you and treat you right. Don't settle for anything less.

Men, it's time to step it up!

12

IS IT OK TO DATE MULTIPLE PEOPLE?

As an adolescent, I was very rambunctious. I was always looking for a way to stir up some mischief. One time, I talked my parents into letting my friends and I turn our backyard into a massive slip-n-slide. Given our nature, once it was set up and ready to roll, we pushed it to the extreme, trying every stunt we could think of. At one point, my mom came running out right as we were about to try to run and slide down the tarp all at the exact same time.

What we, in our youth and naivety, saw as an adventurous challenge, my mom saw as an expensive hospital bill. My mom shouted, "Boys, stop that! Only one at a time!" In hindsight, I realize my mom really kept us from a catastrophe. The entire group had a blast and no one was hurt, simply because of my mom's instruction: "Only one at a time!"

There are so many benefits to healthy dating. It's one of life's greatest explorations. Yet, as it is with any great exploration, it's marked with challenges.

God's plan for this thing called "dating" is rarely clear. He purposely hides His plan like treasure, so you have to find them. They won't just show up at your front door.

So, how do you sort through the masses and find your true love? You could try a million different options that could bring about a million different results. So, if you're asking, "Should I be dating multiple people?" the answer is, "No." But, if you're asking, "Should I go on dates with different people?" the answer is, "Yes!"

In this scenario, my mom's words could not be truer. Whether it's dating or going on a date, you need to do it "one at a time." If you do it any differently than this, someone's going to get hurt.

Humans, for whatever reason, seem to be entertained by bad romances. Think about it. How many movies have you watched that have a love triangle, where an individual "falls in love" with two different people? While some find this entertaining on the big screen, in real life this set up always turns into a big mess.

Here's the deal. When we think of the term "dating," we think of couples. For example, if someone said, "Caleb and Ali are *dating*," we take that to mean: Caleb and Ali are a couple. But, if someone said, "Caleb is *going on a date* with Ali," that doesn't mean Caleb and Ali are a "thing." It just means they're testing the waters, getting to know one another.

If you are in a relationship, you should not be dating multiple people. This isn't wise—or classy. However, from what we've seen, we believe it's best to initially date different people for an extended period of time, before considering long-term dating or locking into a relationship with anyone.

Don't limit yourself to the easiest catch when there could be better options all around you. There is a lot of truth to the old saying: "There are plenty of fish in the sea." Before you become an item with anyone, go out to lunch with different people. Get to know others. You might be grabbing coffee with someone on Monday and going to the movies with someone else on Friday. As long as you are approaching these as a single person who's "going on a date," you've devised a good game plan. This is the perfect way to determine if the person you went out on a date with is someone you are interested in "dating." However, to do it successfully, you need to do it "one at a time."

13

CAN LONG-DISTANCE RELATIONSHIPS WORK?

This question varies for every age bracket. If you are too young to legally marry, don't waste your time. The odds are not in your favor, and the chances of your relationship lasting more than two weeks are slim to none. However, if you are at the age that you could legally marry, then the answer is: Yes, long-distance relationships *can* work, but they are incredibly difficult. One thing is for sure about long-distance relationships: The distance between the two of you cannot be long-term. If you are up for a challenge, you might be able to make it work. First, there are three questions you need to answer when it comes to dating long-distance:

1. **Do you have a plan for spiritual growth?**

    We believe one of the most crucial ingredients for success in dating is the local church. Obviously, when it comes to a long-distance relationship, this can be a bit difficult. If the relationship progresses towards marriage, being in the same church is non-negotiable. This is the first place you really need to start merging your lives. However, in the beginning stages of a long-distance relationship, you have to find other solutions.

How are you and your date going to move forward in your walk with Christ? You need a plan. In the twenty-first century, there are plenty of ways you can stay on the right track:

- *Buy a devotional that you and your date can study together.*
- *Find sermon audio that you can both listen to.*

There are tons of resources!

Then, make it a point once a week to discuss your takeaways from the material you have been covering.

Spiritual growth doesn't just happen. If you do not plan for growth, you will not grow.

2. Can you trust them?

We've all heard the old saying: "Absence makes the heart grow fonder." It's true! But, that's not all it does. It can also make the heart grow jealous, envious, and skeptical.

Long-distance relationships can be very difficult in the arena of trust. Space can easily create speculation.

We all read in between the lines. The biggest problem with reading in between the lines is that we most often read our fears into the situation. An unanswered phone call can quickly escalate from, "He's running behind at work," to, "I bet he's out with his secretary."

For the health of the relationship, if things are going to work, you must be able to quickly move past this hurdle. If you are not confident that the person you are dating can be trusted, you need to stop dating them. Otherwise, you will spend most days frustrated and fearful, thinking that something is going on behind your back.

Are you in this kind of relationship? If so, call it quits. Don't put yourself through the misery. The relationship will not survive. Don't carry around a corpse; bury it, and move on.

3. Do you have the resources to invest in quality time?

You may spend most days separated by many miles, but at some point you've got to close the chasm and spend time together. Amidst all the technological advancements of our day, there is still no replacement for time spent with your significant other in person.

Quality time is irreplaceable. Unfortunately, it can also be fairly expensive. There are two key components that must be considered when talking about long-distance relationships: the costs of travel and time off. Can you financially afford to take time away from work? How often will your employer allow you time off? Can you cover the expenses of fuel or airfare? What about food and lodging? Do you have all that covered?

If you are going to do it right, long-distance relationships can be a bit pricey. This is sure to test the validity of your commitment to the relationship. If you really believe the person you are seeing is worth the investment, then there is no price too high. However, if you do not foresee a future with your date, save your time, money, and energy. Don't burn through your resources investing in something that is going to inevitably collapse. You could miss a better opportunity tomorrow by making the wrong investment today.

We want to finish by saying, over the years we have known a handful of couples who have had long-distance relationships that went on to have very strong marriages. They all agree that dating someone who lives far away can be very difficult. However, they are proof that it can be done.

If you have found someone who is worth the effort, pay the price and make it work. Again, remember, to have a successful long-distance relationship, the distance between the two of you cannot be long-term.

14

DOES ONLINE DATING WORK?

Our world is growing increasingly more digital. From smart phones to tablets, you can stay virtually connected to almost anyone at any time.

This throws a curve ball into the method our grandparents used in dating. No offense, Grandma, but times have changed!

No longer do you have to wait until you are sitting across from your date at dinner to learn about their life. As a matter of fact, you could easily know all about their family, education, work history, and so forth by simply prowling around on the Internet. Meeting someone new has never been easier. The entire world is just one click away.

But, while the Internet certainly has its perks, it is not void of problems. Online dating has become a massive industry. If you are 18 or older and are looking to give it a shot, there are some things you need to know.

Here are the top five liabilities of online dating:

1. **It can be dangerous.**

    Sexual predators are not just lurking the streets; they are online and are often disguised, making appealing offers. This is our greatest concern with online dating.

    In cyberspace, the truth is, you cannot be safe enough. If you find someone on a dating site that you are interested in, do not—under any circumstance—meet with them alone. Once you've found a friend who will tag along, only agree to meet in a very public place.

    Lastly, follow this model the first several times you meet, just in case they are only trying to appease your safety precautions, so they can get you alone and make a move. Do not let your guard down. If the person you are interacting with begins making excuses once you tell them your conditions, end the conversation. They are up to no good.

2. **It can be farfetched.**

    Many online dating sites assure you that they can find you a perfect match. However, putting two people together just because they like sushi, enjoy long walks on the beach, and both like animals doesn't mean they are going to be compatible. Once you get involved in online dating, you need to double down on your dose of "reality."

Think about it.

You have someone sitting behind a screen comparing the likes and dislikes of two individuals, hoping to pair them up in a bright, successful relationship. There is far more chemistry involved in successful relationships than just likes and dislikes.

Their claims may sound optimistic, but they can often be farfetched. While online dating can be a decent starting point for some, don't get discouraged if you discover that it does not work for you.

3. It can be misleading.

We all know someone who has an absurdly misleading profile picture. It is absolutely amazing what a couple of effects and the right camera angle can do. Online dating is no exception. People always put their best foot forward online. You may be shocked when you discover that the handsome young man you were chatting with the other day—the one with those rich, wavy, black locks—has not updated his profile picture in three years. His hair has since gone on vacation and has yet to return.

The point is: Whether it's a misconstrued picture or an exaggerated portfolio, people (especially on dating sites) have a tendency to "stretch" the truth. It's part of the risk you have to take if you are going to get involved in online dating.

Beware: What you see on your computer may clash with who you meet in person.

4. It can be debilitating.

Do you remember, as a little kid, the fear you had of ordering your own food? Thankfully, if your parents were anything like ours, you were forced to step out of your comfort zone and grow up. Otherwise, you would have become socially impaired, always needing others to speak on your behalf.

This is one of online dating's biggest problems. If you aren't cautious, it can be debilitating. If you choose to go down the path of online dating, be very deliberate to not lose the ability to meet new people in person. You do not want to grow dependent on Internet-based dating. You need to be able to ask someone for their name, number, and relationship status in person without fainting. It may seem old-fashioned, but chivalry is not dead.

5. It can be degrading.

Think about this scenario. Pretend you just registered on an online dating site. Your profile picture and personal information has all been entered, and you are ready for business. On the other side of town, there is guy scrolling through profiles, hunting for a potential date. He sees one lady and thinks, "I don't like her hair color," and moves to the next one. He looks at the next picture and thinks, "Too many freckles. Next."

Then, he comes to yours. Knowing nothing about you, he finds something about your picture he doesn't like and moves on. Does that feel a bit degrading?

The idea of scrolling through a list of people until you find what you like can easily warp your paradigm of humanity. Human beings are not mere "products" that you place in a shopping cart for possible purchase. If you start getting involved with online dating sites, be intentional about guarding against a "shopper's" mentality. People are not products.

We want to wrap up by saying that online dating is full of pros and cons. We know people on both ends of the spectrum. One couple we know met online, and they now have a strong, happy marriage. Then, we have other friends who have had atrocious experiences with online dating. If you're already involved in online dating—or are planning on getting involved with an online dating site—use the principles above, and proceed with caution.

15

WHAT CLOTHES ARE APPROPRIATE TO WEAR TO IMPRESS SOMEONE?

The way you dress speaks volumes about you. Our entire lives, we have heard, "You can't judge a book by its cover." This old saying holds significant truth in many arenas of life. However, dating is not one of them.

We want to challenge you to do the exact opposite. People are visual. Our first impression is nearly always based upon what we see. Because of this reality, the way we dress and how we present ourselves is unbelievably important.

A few years ago, a girl came to us seeking relationship advice. She could not understand why every guy she dated ultimately had one agenda: sex. Heartbroken, she said, "Why can't I just find someone who loves me for who I am without wanting my body?"

Sadly, this girl came from a broken home, had poor examples of morality, and was simply modeling what had been modeled to her. There was one primary reason she could not get a man of integrity to show interest in her: Her apparel was attracting the wrong crowd. While this girl genuinely had a heart of gold, her choice in clothing conveyed a much different message.

"Daisy Dukes" and revealing tops may catch the attention of a good man, but it will not keep it. Why? Because a person of integrity resists any opportunity that could potentially cost them their purity.

Ever heard the phrase: "Dress the part"? It means to dress appropriately for the occasion. That's the key. If you want to attract someone of integrity and purity, then dress for that.

You must know these three key principles when it comes to the dating standard on dress:

1. **Modest really is hottest.**

   For too long, modesty has had a bad rap. It is not boring or mediocre—nor is it anti-fashion. If your choice of clothing is terrible, it's not because of modesty; it's because of you. Men, what does your outfit say about you? Find your style and wear it with respect. Ladies, show the world that beauty does not negate clothing. True beauty does not have to show off skin. A revealing outfit is simply the result of an inward cry for attention. You are not cheap eye-candy. You are fearfully and wonderfully made!

2. **If they do not value themselves, they will not value you.**

    We have all been caught off guard by someone in revealing attire. How do you respond to this kind of sexual appeal?

    The deal seems flattering upfront. The pedal is to the floor, but before long you'll realize this vehicle has no brakes. It is certain to crash.

    There is only one reason people dress to appeal to others' sexual appetite: They value someone else's opinion more than they value the opinion they have of themselves. Sadly, this typically stems from past hurts and low self-esteem. Anyone who does not value their purity will not value yours either.

3. **If everyone else is doing it, then you probably shouldn't be.**

    Compromise has been excused far too many times by the logic of, "If everyone else is doing it, then it must be ok."

    The value of something is often based upon its rarity. Do you want to be significant in a sexualized generation? Be unique, don't follow the crowd.

Men, stop trying to justify why it is ok to strut your stuff. Ladies, swimming pools are not an excuse to get undressed in public.

If you are going to do what everyone else does, you are going to get what everyone else gets. You will have to settle for mediocrity when you were made for so much more.

In 2 Corinthians 6, Paul instructs the Church to come out from among the world and be separate. What better place to practice this command than in the realm of dating and purity? Let's go for it!

If we choose to set a standard now, generations to come can avoid the struggles that we have had to endure. We can be the generation that turns the tide. The current social norm could become obsolete in our lifetime if we will take a stand!

16

WHAT ARE APPROPRIATE PLACES TO GO ON A DATE?

During the formative years of our relationship, this was one of our premier questions. Time after time, we would go to a mentor for advice, and they nearly all said the same thing: "Wherever you go, go with a group."

While we highly encourage this ourselves, we quickly discovered that this advice is easier said than done. Within the first few weeks of our efforts to only date in a group setting, we realized that organizing a group for every outing is nearly impossible. While your life may revolve around your relationship, no one else's does.

Secondly, as a couple, we didn't want all of our time together being smothered by friends. This presented a real challenge. Nearly everyone we talked to highly discouraged anything other than going out in a group setting. Yet, we knew that a group setting would never grant us the liberty to really learn about one another.

So, how did we do it?

We decided that if we were going to have a date outside of a group setting, it had to be in public. Otherwise, we knew that we were setting ourselves up for failure.

In dating, never allow privacy to jeopardize purity. One moment alone can escalate much quicker than you anticipate. Regardless of how "strong" you think you are; if you value your purity, you must avoid privacy.

Specifically, when you are at an age that marriage is legally an option, dating takes a major turn. At this phase, having time to really learn about the person you're dating is crucial and, as we stated, can't fully be discovered if you only date in a group. If you're going to date effectively and appropriately, you've got to have some guidelines. Whether you're going in a group or just as a pair, we've got you covered.

Here are three categories (with examples) of ways we kept our dating vibrant, memorable, and appropriate:

1. **Category: Fun.**

   Group: You have tons of options in this category. One of the best ways to practice this is through church events. When we first started dating, our church took a trip to an ice skating rink each winter. We always had a blast on these trips! This gave us a perfect opportunity to connect with each other and our church family.

Individually: It is vitally important to discover your compatibility in this area. If your relationship progresses beyond dating into marriage, you'll quickly discover that the ability to have fun with your significant other is a crucial component to a happy relationship.

We've tried a million different things, creating countless memories along the way. Whether it be a Friday night out bowling or an afternoon trying to long board, fun times shared between you and your date are essential.

2. **Category: Informative.**

Group: Just a few weeks after our first date, we went hiking with a group of friends in the Great Smoky Mountains. The highlight of this date wasn't the breathtaking waterfall we reached at the end of the hike—though it was well worth the walk. The most valuable take-away from this adventure was the discussion along the way.

In a group of friends, you'll find more liberty to speak more openly about your beliefs and preferences. Because of the conversation we all had during the hike, we left knowing far more about one another than we did when we began.

Use such settings as an opportunity to find out who the person you are pursuing really is.

Individually: We are the coffee shop generation, right? This is a perfect way to get some time together, one-on-one, without putting your purity at risk. You need to find ways to interact with your date without the pressure of a group.

Use this time to ask about personal goals:

- *Where do you want to be in five years?*
- *What are your dreams?*

Our local coffee shop became the go-to place for us, especially during our first few years of dating.

3. **Category: Sophisticated.**

    Group: Plan a special group event that requires sophistication. One of our favorite memories comes from our senior prom. We were aware of the traditions on prom night and wanted to avoid that temptation altogether. So, we planned ahead and spent the entire evening with a group of friends.

    From head to toe, everyone was dressed in their finest—something that matters more to the ladies than most guys will ever understand. The reality is, when people dress up, they act differently. It's good to let your date see how you are in your finest. Use a special occasion of this nature as an opportunity to enjoy time with your date and your friends in a formal setting.

Individually: For our two-year dating anniversary, we put on our best and spent the evening at an elegant restaurant in town. We wanted to reflect on the value of our first two years together in a more sophisticated setting. This meant we needed a place that would not allow us to compromise our purity yet afforded us the opportunity to be sappy without being the center of attention.

That can get awkward!

Guys, here's what we recommend: Plan at least one special occasion a year where you've saved up some money to take your lady out for a nice dinner, to remind her how valuable she is to you. You can do this safely by finding a public setting that offers just enough space to keep it from getting weird.

With a little practice and by using these guidelines, you can make the most out of any date whether it be just the two of you or an entire group. You don't have to compromise to enjoy that special someone's company. If you'll use these guidelines now, you can avoid a pitfall later.

17

HOW CAN MY DATE AND I GROW TOGETHER SPIRITUALLY?

If you're asking this question, you're probably heading in the right direction. When it comes to dating, every relationship is doing one of two things to your walk with God: It's either enhancing it or killing it. There is no middle ground. If it's not helping you grow, then it's dead weight and is slowing you down. That's why this question is so significant.

Here are the top five strategies we've found that will help you and your date grow together spiritually:

1. **Keep personal growth top priority.**

    The first goal is not that the two of you would grow as a couple; it's simply that you would grow as individuals. Spiritually, if you don't take care of yourself first, then you can't be of any value to anyone else.

Take time every day to study the Word, seek God in prayer, and meditate upon His goodness. If Jesus is truly the center focus in your individual life, then it will help you and your date keep Him as the center focus in your relationship. If you want to grow together, you must first grow independently.

2. **Don't let relational devotion replace personal devotion.**

We've not only seen countless others slip into this trap, we fell into this one ourselves. While we do highly encourage devoting a portion of the time you spend with your date to studying the Bible or praying together with a group of friends, you cannot let this take the place of your personal time alone seeking God.

We were given a couples' devotional that was phenomenal. Initially, it seemed to give our relationship a fresh jolt in the right direction. But within a few weeks, we both found ourselves growing numb. After praying about it, we both came together to discover that it was simply because we had allowed our personal pursuit of God to be replaced by our devotional time spent together. Your relational devotion should be a supplement not a replacement.

3. **Find resources that you can use together.**

   Once you are secure independently, take advantage of the tools that are available, such as this book, which can help you grow together. In this day and age, you have no excuse for a lack of devotional tools. Ministries all across the world have made resources available at little to no cost.

   When we were dating—and even still today—we'd often watch sermon archives from different church websites instead of movies.

   You've got a myriad of different choices: Download podcasts, buy books, attend conferences, and the list goes on and on. Then, use the content you get, from whichever source you have chosen, as discussion material between you and your date. This practice is an incredible source of strength and growth for all who participate.

4. **Stay connected and committed to the local church.**

   If you want to grow together spiritually, it is essential that you are underneath the same pastor, hearing the same teaching, and are connected to the same church community. We know there are exceptions to the rule, but this is one of the reasons we firmly believe in being planted in the same church if you find your relationship is getting serious. You and your date will naturally grow with much more ease if you are drawing from the same source.

Otherwise, when the two of you are drawing from separate sources, you will find that you are at two totally different phases of development. This can cause great tension and a lack of clarity within the relationship. If things seem to be seriously progressing, getting plugged into the same local church is essential for the life and health of the relationship.

5. Find mentors to disciple you in your relationship.

We quickly found that one of the greatest assets we could have were mentors who modeled the kind of relationship we hoped to have. Thankfully, there were a few couples in our local church who were older than us—some married and some still just dating—who were willing to take us under their wings. We had invaluable takeaways from the times we spent with these couples.

Who do you know that has a healthy relationship you admire? Invite them and their significant other out to lunch, pay for their meals, and let them teach you what they've learned on their journey. This is one of the most valuable resources you can find to assist you in spiritual growth with your date.

These proven principles can help you stay on the right track. Take some time to consider each one and determine ways you can improve upon and implement these into your relationship.

When using these as a guide for spiritual growth, if you discover that your date isn't as serious about growing together as you are, don't try to force it. You need to be with someone who is moving at the same pace. If they aren't interested, they'll become dead weight in your personal walk with God—something you cannot afford.

Spiritual growth is a serious matter. When it comes to dating, make it your highest aim to please the Lord in your relationship.

18

HOW MUCH TIME IS TOO MUCH TIME?

Someone wrote us asking, "According to my parents, my date and I spend too much time together. How much time is too much?"

Let's just start by saying this situation stinks.

All you want is to spend time with your date. Nothing else matters to you right now. We know! I mean c'mon, . . . Why do your parents want to ruin your life anyway?

Ever thought that before?

We sure did. We could not understand why spending every moment of our free time together was a problem. Though our younger selves would cringe to hear us admit this now, we've gotta say: Our parents were right! It must be true; hindsight really is twenty-twenty.

Here are three reasons you should not spend all of your time with the person you are dating:

1. **Spending too much time together can weaken your standard of purity.**

   To build any relationship, you must be willing to invest your time into it. However, if you invest too much time, you'll find that your investment has drained you of some of your most vital resources.

   One of those resources is sound judgment. If you spend enough time with anyone, you'll start to get comfortable with them. Once you get comfortable, you are willing to let your guard down.

   Especially in dating, once your guard is down, temptation can slip right past your standard of purity. When you are sharing so much of your life together, you start, subconsciously—or for some, it may even be consciously—thinking, "Well, I do everything else with them; I guess this wouldn't be that bad," or, "We've kissed a million times and nothing has ever happened before; it won't hurt if we kiss lying down."

   Then, one thing leads to another.

   Before you realize it, you are in a position you never dreamed you would be in—and it all stems back to how much time you've been spending together.

2. Spending too much time together can kill the fire in your relationship.

Spending too much time together can quickly result in a casual approach towards your relationship.

Just like everything else in life, the longer you have it, sadly oftentimes, the less you value it.

Before hanging out with your date, a good question to ask yourself is, "Why are we getting together?" If you are consistently responding to this question with, "Just to hang out," then you are setting your relationship up for failure.

You'll slowly lose interest in the one who used to interest you the most. Rather than just getting together to be together, be intentional. Instead of doing the same old thing three nights in a row, take a couple of nights apart and then go out on a really nice date.

As much as we hated hearing it back then, the truth is, absence really does make the heart grow fonder. You can accomplish more by doing less.

Here's our advice: Spend less time together and make the time you are together really count!

3. **Spending too much time together can cost you friends and family.**

    Remember who was in your life *before* this relationship? They are still there, and they still matter!

    We almost blew it in this area. It's not that we didn't care about our friends and family anymore. It's just that we didn't care as much about them as we did about each other. We were love drunk!

    There's just one problem with being intoxicated by young love—even it leaves a nasty hangover once it wears off. You don't want to invest all of your time into a relationship, lose all your friends, and then a few months down the road discover that the relationship isn't going to work anyways.

    Where will you turn? You've lost all your friends and have made your family feel like you don't value them. Regardless if you are with the one you will one day marry or not, we cannot stress how important it is to avoid sacrificing friends and family for a dating relationship. The ones who were there before Mr. or Mrs. Right will be the ones who are there after them, as well. Don't lose the ones who matter most due to a relationship that may not last.

The truth is, when you find the right one, you don't have to sacrifice others to accommodate them. Don't settle until that's the one you find.

We hope you will take these three points to heart. Time is a finite resource. Once it's gone, you cannot get it back. Make sure you invest it wisely.

Now, go make it count!

19

HOW MUCH SHOULD I TELL MY PARENTS ABOUT MY RELATIONSHIP?

Now, this is a question we get asked a lot! *"My parents are nosey. How much should I tell them about my relationship?"*

You might have even experienced this scenario before.

To answer this question, you have to ask yourself, "How successful do I want this relationship to be?" In most cases, parents aren't too fond about their child's date in the first place. In their eyes, no one will ever be good enough for their son or daughter.

If you are looking for a strong and healthy dating relationship, you've got to prove your parents wrong. You *and* your date have to show them why this relationship is a good thing.

The key to this is transparency.

If you are looking for a successful relationship, you must be transparent. Have you ever heard the old saying:

"If Momma ain't happy, ain't nobody happy?" It's true. If you want to keep Momma happy, you need to answer her questions before she even asks them.

For example, if you are taking someone's daughter on a date, don't wait on the parents to ask you what movie you are going to see, who all will be involved, and what time you are going to have their daughter home. Start by saying, "I'd like to take your daughter to see this new release on a double date with our friends, Chad and Lisa. If it is ok with you, I will have her home at 9 p.m." By doing this, you have shown her parents that you have nothing to hide.

A parent hates nothing more than someone acting suspicious with their child. You have to make it your goal to disarm them of their questions. If they do have other concerns and ask you some questions, just kindly and honestly answer them. Avoiding them and dancing around their questions is a sure sign that you shouldn't be with their son or daughter. If your date's parents feel that you are acting sneaky, it will come at the expense of these three things:

1. **The parents' trust.**

    Think about it. Let's pretend that *you* are a parent. How would you feel if your child was in a relationship that you knew little to nothing about?

If you were a mom or dad and some guy drops by to pick up your daughter without saying a word to you, then you are going to think he is up to no good—and he probably is!

Of course, you would not trust someone like that!

Even for those of you who are shy, when it comes to building trust, you are going to have to press past your timidity and establish a functional relationship with your date's family.

If your date still lives at home with their parents, this is all the more important. While living under the same roof, the parents have more access to your date's ears. Unless you want your relationship to fall apart, you want to make sure their parents think highly of you; they will let their child know their opinion, be it good or bad.

2. **The privilege of freedom.**

While this principle fades the older you get, it is still unbelievably important for all ages. If you want to have the liberty to go on a date without having parents staring over your shoulder, spend time proving that you can be trusted.

This starts by eliminating surprises. You do not want a mom or dad to be surprised by what you are doing with their child.

For example, if your date's parents find out that you hung out with their son or daughter behind their back, you can forget about them letting their child go on a date with you this weekend.

Freedom in dating is not a right; it's a gift, and it must be earned. Unless you establish a clear line of communication where your date's parents know they can ask you anything at any time, they will not trust you with their child. If you want freedom, you need to prove that you can be trusted with it. In the eyes of a good parent who cares about their child, you are guilty until proven innocent.

3. **The parental relationship.**

One of the greatest keys we discovered early in dating was that if we were going to have a strong relationship with one another, we needed to have a strong relationship with each other's parents.

This seems a bit counter-cultural. Movies often depict individuals who hate their date's parents.

But if you approach your date and their mom and dad with respect, you might be surprised to find that some of the richest relationships you have in this life are with them. Don't give them a reason not to like you. Go out of your way to make sure they are involved in your relationship. Keep them in the loop. If you want to have a successful relationship, you must invest in both your date *and* their parents.

Putting transparency into practice at the beginning of the relationship may feel a little uncomfortable; but if you will commit to it from the start, it will become easier over time. You will find the reward well worth the effort.

The more you let your parents in, the more liberty, in time, they will trust you with. Be smart, be open, and prove you are someone who can be trusted.

20

I CAUGHT MY DATE CHEATING. SHOULD I TAKE THEM BACK?

The opportunity to cheat has never been easier. It's no longer just about what you do in person. With the rise of social media, most people are virtually accessible to anybody from anywhere.

This blessing comes with its curses. One, being that in the relationships that are formed online, there is little to no accountability. You can cheat on your significant other by the simple click of a mouse. This means that now more than ever transparency must be a non-negotiable trait in every relationship.

Are you the victim of someone's unfaithfulness?

Whether it happened online or in person makes no difference. Cheating is cheating. When someone you care about betrays you, the pain you experience can seem unbearable.

So, now what?

Do you pretend it never happened and hope things go back to normal? Do you focus on the good and try to ignore the bad? Do you chalk it up as a mistake?

Regardless of the excuse they may give, know this: Cheating is not a mistake; it's a choice.

When children get caught doing something wrong, they immediately cry, trying to save face, "I'm sorry!" Have you ever seen this? It's not uncommon to hear a frustrated mom or dad respond to their child by saying, "Are you sorry for what you did or are you sorry you got caught?"

When someone is caught cheating, they, like the child from the example, tend to show great remorse. Sadly, their sorrow is usually not because of what they did, but because they got caught. Typically, people who cheat, end up apologizing to someone who is emotionally vulnerable and brokenhearted. This is unfortunate because the one that was cheated on often accepts the apology and tries to move forward with the person who was caught cheating.

If you are facing this kind of situation, you need to know three things:

1. **Trusting them will always be a chore.**

    Have you ever heard the phrase, "Out of sight, out of mind?" If you continue dating someone who has cheated on you, you will always be uncomfortable with them being out of your sight; and this can be taxing on your mind. You'll find yourself paranoid with thoughts of them cheating again.

When trust in a relationship has been broken, it doesn't heal easily. We always want to hope for the best. Yet, the truth is, if someone is cheating on you in dating, it's unlikely they will remain faithful in marriage. The problems you are facing right now could be a warning sign of the danger that's ahead if you continue on this road.

Our advice? Without question, if you have caught your date cheating, break it off and leave them behind.

2. You deserve better.

It's not uncommon to face insecurities and feelings of inadequacies when you find out that you have been cheated on.

If you have been the victim of someone's poor decision of unfaithfulness, you may have questioned your worth, asking questions like: "Am I not good enough?" or, "Am I not pretty enough?"

If you have had these thoughts, we need you to know something. Your worth is not determined by their decision. You are far too valuable to stay in a relationship that leaves you feeling inadequate and insecure. You deserve better! Don't settle for a relationship that always leaves you feeling on the edge.

When you say, "Yes," to someone who has been unfaithful to you in the past, you are saying, "No," to someone who could genuinely treasure you in the future.

You don't put real diamond rings in quarter machine toy cases, and neither should someone of value be surrounded by something so cheap. You are worth more than a cheap, unfaithful date!

3. You could become overtly jealous.

When you continually battle the fear of being cheated on, you fall into a dangerous trap. If this kind of insecurity exists, every time someone so much as looks toward your date, you'll interpret it as flirting. This gets real old real quick.

Do you really want to live your life feeling like the only way to keep your significant other from being unfaithful is by putting them on a leash? Do you want to feel obligated to "claim your property" every time the two of you are around others?

As miserable as this sounds, there are countless individuals who live like this day-in and day-out for one simple reason: They are afraid the person who cheated on them before will cheat on them again.

If you are in this kind of relationship, don't get stuck. A healthy relationship is possible! If you are battling intense jealousy, always trying to claim what's yours, it's time to move on!

If you have been on the other side of this scenario, where you have been the one cheating, dating isn't for you. You can't go from person to person, toying with their hearts and emotions. Until you have enough respect, not just for your date but for yourself, you have no business trying to get into a relationship.

On the other hand, if you have blown it and genuinely regret it, we've got good news. There is hope! There are three crucial steps to moving forward.

First, repent. Ask God to forgive you for living in a way that is not pleasing to Him.

Second, apologize to the person you cheated on. This will no doubt be uncomfortable. You are not apologizing to restore the relationship. The relationship is done. You are apologizing because you messed up.

The final step is making a quality commitment to yourself before God, that you will never cross that line again.

When you truly value yourself and others, the idea of cheating on your date has no appeal. Your name is too valuable. If you are going to date, make sure you do it right. Don't run your name through the mud by succumbing to an opportunity that is below your character.

Even more so, as a believer, you are carrying a name far greater than your own and far greater than your date's. You are carrying the name of Christ. Make sure you carry His name well.

21

WHAT'S THE BEST WAY TO BREAK UP WITH SOMEONE?

Ending a relationship is never fun, unless you are cold and heartless. Yet, life happens, and it has to be done. If you have ever been on the negative end of a break up, you know that there is a right way and a wrong way to end things.

Here are ten ways you should never break up with someone:

1. **Never say, "God told me it's time to break up with you."**

   While it is true that God might tell you that you need to end a relationship, using the "God told me" card is not the best way to handle it.

   For starters, what does this communicate to the person on the other end? Does God think you're better than them; and consequently, He wants you to end it? This could easily give your ex, especially someone who's young in the faith, a misleading view of who God really is.

Secondly, chances are, if you are hearing God tell you to get *out* of the relationship, He probably never told you to get *into* the relationship. This means you need to be an adult and bear the brunt of your decision.

2. Never say, "It's not you; it's me."

Breaking up is messy. It's never easy. When you try to soften the blow, you typically make matters worse. Everyone knows that this old break-up line is simply a cover-up.

If you are not emotionally prepared to end a relationship, then you should have never begun one. Breaking up doesn't have to be done heartlessly. Be classy and honest. That's the best way to face the challenge.

3. Never say, "I see you as more of a friend."

Again, this just comes down to needing a cover-up. Why do you want to break up? Are you no longer attracted to them? While you should not tell your date that they've lost their physical appeal, lying is just as bad. The truth of the matter is, you are not obligated to give them an in-depth reason for ending the relationship. Out of courtesy, you ought to give some explanation, but it doesn't have to be detailed.

4. **Never get a friend to end your relationship.**

   If you're in middle school, this may still be acceptable; but if you want to handle things like an adult, then your break-ups shouldn't include a third party. Would it be easier to not face the awkward situation? For sure! But if you are going to be a person of character and integrity, you've got to handle this situation, not your friends.

5. **Never break up in public.**

   It's already going to be painful enough, but breaking up with someone in front of other people is like rubbing dirt in an open wound. You are not aiming to make the situation any worse than it already has to be. If you find that people are around whenever you plan to end the relationship, then postpone your plans and aim for the next available moment. Turn the tables and imagine being dumped by someone you really care about in front of other people. You would be humiliated, right? We all would. Do it without a bunch of people present.

6. **You should never break up over text.**

   If you don't care about your reputation and you just want a quick easy way out, this method is perfect for you. Hopefully, that's not the case, and you are a person of strong character and integrity. If so, this method is not for you.

   People who break up over text are typically just looking out for themselves. They don't want to deal with any more pain than necessary.

   Here's the deal. Breaking up isn't easy, nor should it be. Ending a relationship is not something that we should approach casually, even if it's long overdue. You should have enough respect for both yourself and the person you've been with to handle a break-up with character. If you are going to call it quits, do it face-to-face.

7. **Never try to let it die slowly.**

   First, you ignore their calls. Then, you "get called into work," and before you know it you're using whatever excuse you can think of to avoid them.

   You can quickly find yourself running from the person you once ran to. If you have become emotionally detached from the relationship, don't try to drag the commitment out.

   First, it's not fair to them; and second, you'll be miserable. Sometimes people try to let the relationship die slowly because they genuinely don't want to hurt the other person. Unfortunately, it's inevitable. It's how the dating world is designed. You must have the strength to close the curtain when the show is over, even if it hurts. Remember dating isn't marriage; it's ok to get out of the relationship.

8. **Never try to get them to break up with you.**

    So, you're too scared to throw in the towel, but you want out. What do you do? Do you let your date catch you sending flirty text messages to other people? What if you pick up some annoying habits? You know, things that really irk your date? Since you are too afraid to break up with them, maybe there's something you could do to make your date break up with you.

    Listen—this is completely ridiculous.

    Save yourself the time and energy. As Mother always says, "You got yourself in this mess; you can get yourself out of it." Don't use them as your pawn. Act your age and end the relationship like an adult.

9. **Never say, "I think we should take a break."**

    No matter how much you try to soften the blow, when all is said and done, someone's feelings are going to get hurt. If you really liked the person, you would not want to take a break.

Rather than beating around the bush, call it what it really is. This doesn't mean you have to be rude or heartless, but you can't afford to be misleading. If you are really done, then do not leave them with the hope that there could still be a future together. Don't be passive; be direct. Being open, heartfelt, and honest are the best actions you can offer in this situation.

10. **Never say, "I think we should see other people."**

There are a couple of problems this statement could communicate when breaking up. One, it could communicate that while in your current relationship, you have found someone else you are interested in. This is a major blow to your character. When you are in a relationship, be fully there.

Secondly, it could communicate that you are too weak to explain the real reason you are ready to move on and just wanted a cheap phrase to do the dirty work. Again, this speaks of poor character. If you are going to end the relationship, don't use a cheap copout; just be gentle and honest.

Ending a relationship isn't easy, but don't let the discomfort of the present circumstance leave a lasting blemish on your character. While it may hurt in the moment, the best way to end a relationship is to communicate, through meekness and sincerity, why you are ready to move on. If you were courageous enough to get into the relationship, then guess what? You must be courageous enough to get out of the relationship. This advice will help you end the relationship on terms that will not jeopardize your reputation.

22

CAN I BE FRIENDS WITH MY EX?

So, you had a relationship that didn't go as planned? Welcome to the club. This is where things can get a little bit tricky. If you and your ex share any part of your lives together—maybe you go to the same school, work for the same company, or attend the same church—you're probably asking yourself, "What do I do now?"

Unfortunately, there is no "one size fits all" solution for this challenge. Much of your decision will be based on how your dating relationship with them ended. While there are situations where the most appropriate and beneficial thing to do is to fully sever ties with them, this is not always the case.

It is possible to have a functional relationship with someone you've dated in the past. Yet, it won't be problem-free.

There are four things that could happen when you befriend an ex:

1. **It could get awkward.**

    Whether you like it or not, the truth is, you cannot undo the past. The memories you created and times you shared with your ex aren't going to vanish. If you become friends with an old boyfriend or girlfriend, you will discover that your history with them becomes a shared affinity between the two of you.

    For example, let's say while you were dating, you had a special song. Maybe it was the first song you danced to with them, or it's the song that was playing when you went on your first date. Whatever the case may be, the song was special to the relationship.

    Now we've got to ask: How's it going to feel when you stop by their cubicle at work and that song just so happens to come on the radio while you are standing there?

    Can you say, "Awkward"?

    There are endless opportunities for uncomfortable moments in this kind of friendship. This is one of the many risks you must embrace if you are going to befriend an ex.

2. **It could progress.**

   If you fell for them in the past, what makes you so sure you won't fall for them again in the future? Why did you break up in the first place?

   If you called things off for minor reasons before, getting back together isn't necessarily a bad thing. Maybe you aren't into them at all, and there's no chance you would consider dating them again. Are the feelings mutual? Do they feel the same?

   When you befriend an ex, there's always a chance that they are seeing the friendship through a different lens than you are. They could see it as a stepping stone towards dating again. If this makes you nervous, then bringing your ex back into your life as a friend probably isn't the best idea.

3. **It could cause problems.**

   So, let's say you have moved on. You have been in another relationship for a couple of months now, and you like the way things are going. If you try to befriend your ex, you may find that your current date isn't as enthused about the idea as you are. This could cause your current date to feel like they have to compete with your previous date.

If you really like the person you are dating, we advise you to talk to them about how they would feel if you were to befriend your ex. If they do not feel comfortable with it, you need to ask yourself if it is something you can live with. Can you live without that friendship? If not, you could have some problems. Unless one of you is willing to compromise, your current relationship will be over before you know it.

Befriending an ex can get quite pricey.

4. **It could fail.**

Albert Einstein has been widely credited for saying, "The definition of insanity is doing the same thing over and over again, but expecting different results."

Most often, in what we have seen, failed dating relationships do not make the best friendships. It's typically just the same people getting the same results: Everything is good for a while, then it ends the same way it did before.

It is very difficult to defy the odds. If you are going to have any kind of successful relationship with an ex, it will take a lot of patience and practice. These aren't obstacles you overcome overnight; it will take some time. Remember, we are talking about befriending the person you either dumped or were dumped by. There are a lot of raw emotions involved in this situation. But, if you are both committed to moving forward, who knows? You could be the exception to the rule.

Otherwise, don't be devastated if you discover that there are some things you just can't bounce back from.

If you read all four of these points and still have an optimistic outlook on befriending your ex, then it might be worth a shot. However, before you do, we highly encourage you to re-evaluate why the relationship you had with them ended in the first place. Was it on bad terms? If so, do you really think it would be healthy to get back involved with them?

Don't answer too quickly. Take some time to really pray and seek God about this decision. One bad relationship can produce devastating results. Move slowly and be smart. Good decisions are rarely made in haste. Take your time. You've got to!

23

HOW DO I HANDLE RUMORS FROM A MAD EX?

So, you're in a sticky situation. The way you respond to the rumors about you that have been floating around will either disable the bomb or set it off. We want to help you disable it.

Here's our advice on how to handle rumors being spread by a mad ex:

1. **Talk to a trusted mentor.**

    Each situation is unique. We can't give a generic answer that applies to everyone. Do you want to handle this situation the right way? Seek counsel. When it comes to rumors, you need the advice of someone who's not involved. You need someone who will cheer you on one minute and call you out the next. The goal is not to get someone on your side; the goal is to respond to accusations with integrity.

2. **Decide if you should confront them or ignore them.**

    You've got to weigh the pros and cons. Again, this decision needs to be made under the care of a mentor.

    On one hand, you have to ask: Are the rumors my ex is spreading, from a bad decision I made that I might, unfortunately, have to bear the brunt of for a while? Would saying something rile them up even more?

    On the other hand, you have to ask: Have I instigated some kind of confusion or anger? Would confronting them bring clarity and peace to the situation?

    Ultimately, you want to clear the air. However, at times, the best thing is to patiently wait without causing a scene.

3. **Never fight fire with fire.**

    If someone is gossiping about you, please understand something. That's not your cue to do the same about them. We've seen this scenario far too many times, and the result is always the same: When you fight fire with fire, you only cause the flames to grow. As believers, we do not have to retaliate. We can rest knowing that God is our Defender.

4. **If you need to confront them, wait until you're calm.**

    We do not handle problems the right way when we are angry. This is why you need to take it slow. Blow off some steam first and clear your head.

    Do you want to be really courageous? Before you talk with them, put yourself in their shoes. Think about why they are doing what they are doing and how you can bring peace to the situation. You don't want to make matters worse. To avoid doing so, your gossiping ex needs to see that you are not coming at them with an attack. Work to resolve the issue, not to prove your point.

5. **Stick close to your friends.**

    Do you have people in your life who, even when you are at your worst, choose to see the best in you? These are the people you need to stick with, even more so in these times. In hard situations, the safety of a loyal friend is essential. Everyone needs encouragement and moral support from time to time.

    Here's our advice. Find the people in your life who love you no matter what you are facing and are willing to help you through this challenging situation. Once you've found them, be intentional about letting them know how thankful you are for their friendship.

Finding yourself surrounded by rumors can be a bit intimidating. However, you can win. We believe these principles can help point you toward victory!

24

HOW SHOULD I HANDLE BEING DUMPED?

Being dumped is never easy. Feelings of rejection and inadequacy often ensue after breakups, causing people to question their value. When a relationship ends, you inevitably face the pain and discomfort that comes with it. But, remember, you are in charge of your response.

Here are five key ways to handle being dumped:

1. **Be respectful.**

    When we feel betrayed or hurt by someone, our natural human tendency is to go into defense mode. This is when you retaliate and try to make the person who wounded you feel the same level of pain you feel. Just because it's natural, doesn't mean it's right. As Christians, we do not return slander with slander.

    As tempting as it may be, don't retaliate if you've gone through a rough breakup. You are too good to stoop to such a low level. Lift up your head, look to the future, and move on.

2. **Don't be desperate.**

Do not fight to convince your now-ex that somehow they've made a horrible mistake. If you have to convince someone of your value, they are not worth your time.

Though in the heat of a breakup it may be tough to see, you will find someone who genuinely loves you for who you are without ever having to prove anything. But, you have to be patient and seek the Lord.

If they are running from you, do not chase them. Just wave goodbye.

3. **Turn to friends.**

Bill Withers was right when he said, "We all need somebody to lean on." One of the worst things to do, when going through a breakup, is to try to bear the pain alone. You weren't meant to stand all by yourself under such a heavy load.

Go to those who will hold you up. Please note, we are not saying that you should go to them and trash your ex. But, we are saying that it is important to have people in your life who can comfort you when you're facing difficult circumstances. So, in this situation, turn to your friends.

4. **Take your time.**

   There is a healing process to anything that's been broken, and your heart is no exception. If you get into another relationship, trying to move on from the pain of a previous relationship, you're just setting yourself up for failure. Don't play the rebound game.

   Take time to re-evaluate yourself and your aspirations. What are you looking for in a relationship? Once you are reminded of this, don't settle. You cannot afford to lower your standards. Take time for healing, aim high, and then get back in the game.

5. **Turn to God.**

   More important than anything else, you must turn to the source of all comfort and peace.

   1 Peter 5:7 says, *"Give all your worries and cares to God, for He cares about you,"* (NLT). When it comes to hurt and pain, if it matters to you, then it matters to God. Others may think you are overreacting when you face a breakup, but God knows what you are really facing, even when no one else does. Sure, in time, you'll probably look back and think to yourself, "Man, I made that into a much bigger deal than it really was," but God isn't waiting until you get

through the pain to help you. He wants to help you in every moment, both great and small.

At the time, breakups always seem much bigger than they really are. That's not to belittle you or the pain you might feel when facing such a situation. It's simply to say that, although it seems insurmountable now, you will overcome. Above all, know this: When you keep following God, you can be assured; your future is brighter and better than you've ever imagined!

25

WHAT'S THE BEST WAY TO WORK OUT ARGUMENTS?

Arguments—every couple has them. Sometimes they're about something insignificant, like arguing over where to eat, where to go, or what to do. Other times, you may find yourself in a far more serious argument.

Typically, when it comes to "little" arguments, if you'll just step back for a minute, you will realize that you are arguing over something that doesn't even matter. The solution to this is simple: Esteem your date above yourself. Don't let a little argument take a major toll on your relationship. It's not worth it.

However, when it comes to "big" arguments, the way you handle them is much more complex.

There are three primary solutions when it comes to dealing with arguments in dating:

1. **Agree to disagree.**

   As long as it isn't a moral issue or a matter of personal conviction, you may find that the solution for you and your date is to agree that you do not see eye-to-eye on the matter. In this scenario, you have three options once you've decided to agree to disagree: (1.) You can either compromise and meet in the middle, (2.) sacrifice your preference for theirs, or (3.) postpone the decision-making process until a later time.

   This is *never* the case when it comes to purity or personal conviction. In that instance, you must remain true to your core values—even if it costs you your relationship.

   But, that is not the source of all arguments in relationships. It's easiest to reach a place of resolve when you keep your date's best interests in mind.

2. **Seek help.**

   If you are highly invested in the relationship, this is especially important. With this solution, you have two options.

   The first—and the one we recommend most—is to individually seek advice from a counselor or spiritual leader regarding the matter. Of course in this case, you need to be classy.

You're not just looking to throw your date under the bus and find someone to agree with you. Instead, genuinely seek advice with no ulterior motives.

The second option to this solution is to get help from a spiritual mentor as a couple. We only recommend doing this if you've already met with someone individually, and they suggest a meeting with the two of you. This is especially important when the argument stems from a moral failure or from a relationship that has crossed the lines of personal conviction. Sometimes when two individuals are arguing, the best solution is to get the wisdom of someone who is not involved in the situation and has the liberty to speak unbiasedly to you both.

3. **Break up.**

The truth of the matter is, you are not married. This means if you are unable to reach a place of resolve and the issue you are arguing about is too important to compromise, then you may find that the best solution, though painful, is to pull the plug.

When you're dating, you must remember that you are not obligated to work out the argument. If the root of the issue is something you are not able or willing to budge on, then don't drag out the relationship. Time will not cause the issue to disappear. If it is really that important to you, it will only make it worse. You should not try to continue building a relationship with someone you cannot flow in harmony with. Disagreement is not supposed to be the everyday norm. If this sounds like your situation, break up and move on.

Next time you and your date are facing an argument, we advise you to reflect upon these solutions. If you learn to work out arguments the right way in the beginning of your relationship, then you can avoid a lot of pain and frustration down the road. Take these principles to heart and learn how to properly reach a place of resolve.

26

HOW CAN I KNOW IF MY DATE IS CONTROLLING?

Dating can be done right. When those involved are approaching one another with love and care, the relationship can actually be of great value. However, there are some dating habits that you should watch out for.

If you are concerned that you or someone you know is being controlled by a boyfriend or girlfriend, then read on and take a mental evaluation. Control and abuse go hand-in-hand. There is no room for either in any relationship.

Are you in this kind of relationship?

Here are 10 signs that your significant other is controlling you:

(NOTE: You obviously do not want to wrongfully accuse anyone of being abusive or controlling. Before you bring accusations against anyone, seek help. If any of the following warning signs are present, immediately find someone you

can discuss your concerns with. Do not, under any circumstance, ignore these problems. Get help!)

1. **Do they keep you from friends and family?**

    This is what you call an isolation tactic. Someone who is controlling wants you to spend every minute with him or her, without ever considering what you would prefer. It is normal to want to spend time with your girlfriend or boyfriend; however, it is dangerous to spend an excessive amount of time together in the dating phase. It produces unhealthy boundaries.

    If you are with someone who is controlling, they might try to make you feel bad for wanting to spend time with someone else. They might say things like, "You would rather spend time with your mom than me? I guess you don't love me." Does this happen in your relationship? This tends to be a symptom of control issues.

2. **Do they constantly criticize or belittle you?**

    "You can't do anything right." "You will never be good enough." Someone who is controlling will say things like this to try to make you feel like you are nothing without them. Does your date ever make you have such thoughts? If you feel inadequate without them, you may have fallen right into their trap. They ultimately want to manipulate you into believing that you need them to feel complete and significant. If you are with someone who causes you to feel this way, you need to move on!

3. **Do they intrude on your privacy?**

   A person who wants to control you will have zero respect for your personal space. For example, they may demand the login information to all your social media accounts, so they always know your private conversations. Even worse, they may demand that you share an account with them.

   Another example is someone who always wants to review who you are texting and what's being said. This could be a sure sign that they are struggling with trust and control issues.

4. **Do they keep a detailed record of wrongs?**

   First of all, no one is perfect. We all mess up. Certain mistakes seem to resonate longer than others, and it can be difficult to move on. However, someone with control issues will regularly remind you of past wrongs. Does your date ever say things like, "I can't trust you because you liked that chick's photo three months ago," or, "Remember when you . . . ?" If so, there could be a problem.

You should never allow anyone to define you by your past mistakes. If your boyfriend or girlfriend can't let go of your past mistakes, it's time to let go of them.

5. **Do they use guilt as a tool against you?**

    This is simply a method of manipulation. Controlling people are often selfish people who are looking for personal gain at the expense of others.

    In a relationship, these people will use guilt to get something from you that they want. For example, they may say things like, "If you don't buy me food, I will starve," or even more serious, "If you break up with me, I will hurt myself."

    Never fall prey to their agenda. If someone is threatening to hurt themselves because of something they are requesting of you, they need immediate help. Do not tolerate such manipulation. Turn to someone for professional guidance.

6. **Do they make acceptance conditional?**

    Someone with this negative attribute will say things like, "I will love you if you do this," or, "I won't love you if you wear that . . ." Again, this is a form of manipulation used for personal gain. Anyone who says their love is contingent upon what you may or may not do does not really love you anyway. If your boyfriend or girlfriend is using this weapon against you, get out. They are not worth your time!

7. Do they need a play-by-play?

One of the most common signs among those who have control issues is that they require constant disclosure.

Does your date call you every five minutes to "check-in"? If you are dating someone who always wants to know who you are with and what you are doing when you are away from them, you may be with the wrong person. If they are bothered by the thought of you enjoying life when you are apart, then there is a major issue. Are you with this kind of overly-clingy person?

Pay attention to the warning signs!

8. Do they get overly jealous?

Does your significant other closely monitor your interactions with the opposite sex? Someone who is controlling has deep-rooted insecurities; and because of those insecurities, they get jealous easily.

We are not talking about a healthy jealousy either. For example, we serve a God who is jealous for our love. It is healthy to feel jealous when someone flirts with your guy or gal. However, someone with control issues will take it to the extreme, which is very dangerous. If your significant other does not let you have friends of the opposite sex, including social media friends, then there is an unhealthy jealousy.

9. Do they refuse to hear you out?

A controlling person only cares about his/her own point of view. They refuse to hear you out or come to a place of mutual agreement by compromising their argument.

Are you dating someone who thinks they are always right? Have they ever admitted that they were wrong? Someone with this issue refuses to lose an argument. In their eyes, even when they know otherwise, they are never at fault. If you are dating someone with an "It's my way or the highway" mentality, end the relationship. You deserve better!

10. Do they threaten you?

This may be the most dangerous sign of all. If you are with someone who threatens to end the relationship every time you do something they don't like, you need to end it as soon as possible.

Oftentimes, among those who make these kinds of threats, there is an ill progression. This is why we say this sign is the most dangerous. In stage one, they say things like, "If you do this, I will break up with you." In stage two, they turn it up a notch and say things like, "If you do this, I will hurt you." Our advice: End the relationship at stage one. If you are already in stage two and are receiving threats that could be physically or emotionally harmful, reach out to someone in authority immediately. Do not wait!

These signs are meant to help you discern and avoid unhealthy relationships. If your boyfriend or girlfriend has checked out on any of these signs, then we suggest you break up and move on. People with control issues must confront their problems. If you do not move on, you will find yourself weighed down and lifeless.

We know that sometimes letting someone go is easier in theory than it is in reality. If you are having trouble making the right decision, we encourage you to reach out to someone who can help lead the way.

COULD GOD BE CALLING ME TO BE SINGLE?

Could God be calling you to live single for the rest of your life? Check out what the apostle Paul wrote about that:

"Sometimes I wish everyone were single like me—a simpler life in many ways! But celibacy is not for everyone any more than marriage is. God gives the gift of the single life to some, the gift of the married life to others."

1 Corinthians 7:7 (MSG)

So, again, could God be calling you to live single for the rest of your life? Yes. But did you catch what Paul said?

It's a gift.

Celibacy simply means to abstain from marriage and sexual relations.

Before we go any further, we want to dispel the two most common myths that surround the subject of celibacy.

MYTH #1

BEING CELIBATE DOESN'T MEAN YOU'RE WEIRD.

Remember, it's a calling. Though the concept may be foreign to our culture, it still exists in the Scripture. As a matter of fact, some of the greatest people of the Bible embraced lives of celibacy.

Paul even dared to say:

> *"But I want you to be without care. He who is unmarried cares for the things of the Lord—how he may please the Lord. But he who is married cares about the things of the world—how he may please his wife."*
>
> 1 Corinthians 7:32-33 (NKJV)

Though this doesn't mean that marriage is wrong, it does mean that a life of singleness comes with great advantages for the Kingdom. We must dispel the myth that you are somehow "less than" others or "strange" if you are called to a life of celibacy. It is an honorable call that you need not be ashamed of.

MYTH #2

BEING CELIBATE DOESN'T MEAN YOU STRUGGLE WITH HOMOSEXUALITY.

The second myth to dispel is the idea that those called to celibacy struggle with homosexuality. These are not interchangeable terms that mean the same thing. One does not equal the other. Sadly though, nearly every time we've discussed the call of singleness, we've discovered that many connect it to homosexuality. Just because someone is not drawn to the opposite sex does not mean that they are romantically attracted to the same sex.

To make this claim is to suggest that Jesus, Paul, and many other notable characters were secretly homosexual. Nothing could be further from the truth! Unfortunately, in our culture if you are called to a celibate lifestyle, you will most likely face accusation in this area. But rest assured, the same God who called you will comfort you should persecution arise.

We hope that by dispelling these myths you can see that celibacy is not a bad thing. If you should discover that God has called you to a life of singleness, count it an honor that you've been called by the King!

We have three questions for you to consider when determining whether or not you are called to a life of celibacy:

1. **Do you dread the thought of lifelong celibacy?**

   We can both remember times early in our teenage years when we were riddled with fear, thinking that God could possibly be calling us to a life of celibacy. We were terrified!

   Have you ever felt that way?

   If so, we want to ease your fears. You're not called to celibacy. Here's the deal. As we stated earlier, the call to a life of singleness, as the apostle Paul wrote, is a gift. In James 1:17, it says:

   > *"Every good gift and every perfect gift is from above, and comes down from the Father of lights..."*
   >
   > (NKJV)

   Do you know what this means? If the gift isn't good and perfect, it's not from God. If the "gift" of celibacy would make you miserable, then it's not good, and it's not God!

   We don't serve a King who sits on His throne pondering how He can bring us misery. He didn't look at you and think, "They would hate nothing more than staying single for the rest of their lives, so that's what I'm going to give them."

   No way!

As a Father, He delights in giving you the best. Our pastor has often said that the best theology there is to learn, most of us learned as little children around the dinner table, praying before we ate. You'll remember this prayer:

> "God is great; God is good. Let us thank Him for our food."

It's this simple. If the thought of singleness puts your stomach in knots, that's neither great nor good, and you have no reason to worry about it being from God.

2. Is this a lifetime calling or a seasonal calling?

If you thoroughly believe that God is calling you to a life of singleness, then there are some practical instructions we highly advise. The first step in making a lifetime commitment is making a temporary commitment. You don't want to make a commitment to God that you can't keep. Act soberly.

If you are just coming through a bad breakup where you've decided that all guys are pigs, and you're never dating again, we don't recommend that you make a lifelong commitment to God to live single forever.

Again, act soberly. We suggest that your first commitment of singleness not exceed one year. We don't want you pledging a life of celibacy to God, only to have a complete change of heart a year into your endeavor when Mr. or Ms. Perfect walks in the room.

First, commit a season of your life to singleness where you do not pursue the opposite sex at all, placing all of your affections and pursuits on God alone. After a short-term commitment, seek God in prayer and fasting, re-evaluate your desires, and then soberly move forward.

3. **Do you face strong sexual desires?**

   Sex and celibacy do not go together. If you sense the call to a life of celibacy, you need to know that this means a life of abstinence. While this isn't to say that you will not have any sexual desires, you will find that you can readily take control over such desires. If sex is something you genuinely look forward to, then you're probably not called to celibacy. Here's what Paul had to say about this matter:

   > "... if they cannot exercise self-control, let them marry."
   >
   > 1 Corinthians 7:9b (NKJV)

If you are attracted to the opposite sex, it doesn't mean that something's wrong with you. But it is, however, a strong indicator that you should not make any long-term commitments to live single.

At the public high school we attended, we were privileged to have an Old Testament and New Testament Survey Bible class. When we came to 1 Corinthians 7, our teacher told us of one of his dear friends, an older gentleman, who was genuinely called to a life of celibacy. The man had no strong attraction for women, and neither did he struggle with homosexuality. For several years, in his younger days, he tried to date but no relationship brought satisfaction. He recognized a pretty lady when he saw one, but never had any real desire for her. If you are called to a life of celibacy, this will be true of you, too.

If you find yourself contemplating a life of singleness, use these three questions as a healthy guide. Where God calls us, He equips us. If you are being called to a life of celibacy, though it will come with its sacrifices just as marriage would, it won't be taxing and troublesome. But, rather, you'll find it to be both empowering and invigorating.

If you sense God is calling you to this kind of life, talk to a spiritual leader. Go to your pastor or a spiritual mentor who will encourage and inspire you as you travel forward along this journey!

28

HOW DO I KNOW IF I'VE MET "THE ONE"?

Before you read any further, we need to tell you something. The question you are asking—we asked it, too. However, we discovered there isn't a simple answer. Thankfully, though, we did find some practical keys that pointed us to success.

Here are four key questions you must ask when considering if you should marry the person you are dating:

1. **Is the person you want to marry someone you would be fine living without?**

    When we were going through premarital counseling, our pastors asked us, "How would you feel about living without each other for the rest of your lives?"

    What a question!

Just the thought of this gave us a gnawing pain in the pits of our stomachs.

For many, though, when asked this question, they realized they weren't really as "in love" as they thought they were.

How would you feel if the person you were considering for marriage was no longer a close part of your life? Sure, it would hurt. But, how difficult would it be to move on? If you find that you are continually trying to *convince yourself* that you have found "the one," then they are probably not "the one."

Marriage is a big deal. It is a lifelong, forever commitment. So, of course, you feel a lot of pressure when trying to determine if you've found the one person you want to spend the rest of your life with. But, the thought of living without them should strike a nerve at the core of your being that you cannot suppress. If you could easily live without them, then you probably should.

2. **Does the person you want to marry love someone else more than they love you?**

It may sound cliché or seem overstated, but it is the simple truth. The person you want to marry must be more in love with Jesus than they are with you. This is the most essential part of any vibrant marriage. If you want a marriage that is vibrant, full of vitality, and built to last, then you must make sure the person you are considering has this as their top priority, too. The reality is simply that until they love Jesus more than anyone else, they will never be able to love you, as their spouse, the way you deserve to be loved.

Look for this in dating. Evaluate their passions, and see who truly has their heart. This is the number one secret to every Godly and successful relationship.

3. Is the person you want to marry your best friend?

Every great marriage is built on the foundation of friendship. Our society has painted a very deceptive picture. If you want a happy, healthy marriage, you cannot afford to use your favorite movie or novel as your standard. Hollywood suggests that love is a mere romantic escapade, full of steamy moments. If you let Hollywood set the standard for what you should find in a spouse, you are going to be in trouble. Not every moment in life and marriage is going to look like a scene from a movie.

This is why your relationship must be built on the foundation of friendship. When you face moments that are anything but romantic, the friendship you've found in that person will stand the test. We're not devaluing romance; we're just embracing the real value of friendship and its ability to weather any storm.

So, when you're trying to determine if you have found "the one," you have to ask yourself: "Is this person my best friend?"

4. Is the person you want to marry gracious and merciful?

People always put their best foot forward in dating. This means that if they do not show you grace and mercy in dating, they certainly won't in marriage.

We'll never forget sitting in premarital counseling, listening to our pastors explain to us that there would be moments in marriage where our spouse would get on our last nerve and push us to the edge. They said the things we once thought were cute might all of a sudden drive us crazy.

This is why mercy and grace are essential. Ultimately, you've got to learn to laugh things off.

The last time you and your date had an argument, how did they handle it? Everyone mishandles an argument every now and then.

But if they're never able to just laugh it off and move on, then you really need to proceed with caution.

You do not want to marry someone who is always obstinate, when it comes to extending mercy every time you mess up. In marriage, you cannot afford to take yourself too seriously. You are both human. Mistakes are inevitable, and you're going to come up short from time to time. So, whether it's from a busy day at work or just day-to-day tension, watch how your date handles pressure.

What about the way they respond when you blow it? If it isn't with grace and mercy, then you should not consider marriage with them.

Every successful relationship consists of these four components. Whether you're single, dating, or looking to get married, take note of these principles. Be willing to ask the difficult questions. If the relationship is meant to be, it can stand the test. We must do things right and honor God in this most important relationship called "marriage."

29

HOW DO I KNOW IF I'M IN LOVE?

You can only answer this question if you know what love is. Is love an emotion? Maybe a deep feeling of passion? We've heard many say that they thought they were in love but eventually discovered it was just the flu.

If there has ever been a generation with an inaccurate definition of this most serious matter, it's ours. Something of such immeasurable value cannot be so spontaneous. We cannot afford to see love through the filter of Hollywood any longer. If we are going to have relationships of strength and sustainability, we must return to the Biblical definition of love.

While 1 Corinthians 13 was clearly written around the context of spiritual gifts, it does, nonetheless, give one of the Bible's clearest breakdowns on what love actually is. Using this passage as a guide can help determine if you are actually "in love" or you've just caught the stomach bug. Find out with the eight keys below:

1. **Love is patient and kind.**

    In the early phases of dating, with no real responsibility and very little commitment, this may seem pretty simple. Everything about them is cute, right?

    Just give it some time.

    How well can you handle sustaining this same attitude of patience and kindness when you have bills to pay, dinner to cook, and a house to clean? Can you make the choice to extend this kind of response to the person you "love" when they aren't acting very lovable?

    Because *that* is what true love looks like.

2. **Love does not envy or boast.**

    These two issues are two sides of the same coin. On one side, you have envy, which often looks like a disgruntled spouse, wishing they were in another relationship or—even worse—wishing they had someone else's spouse.

    Then, on the other side, you have boasting, which typically stems from putting too much faith in what you, as a couple, have accomplished compared to everyone else you know.

These two issues both come from one deadly source—comparison. If you compare their bad moments with someone else's good moments, you'll end up with envy. Likewise, if you compare your good moments with someone else's bad moments, you'll end up boasting. Finding contentment where you are and with who you have without comparison is a key factor to consider when answering the question, "Can I love this person?"

3. **Love is not arrogant or rude.**

By definition, "arrogance" is *"having or revealing an exaggerated sense of one's own importance or abilities."*[1] The word "rude" originates from the Latin word *rudis* which means *"unwrought"* or simply put, *"rough."*[2]

The solution to arrogance is authenticity. Be who you are, even if it means exposing some of your flaws. However, as you open up and allow your significant other to see you for who you are, be gentle. We are not encouraging you to be uncouth in the name of authenticity. In love, there is a tension between living authentically, which combats arrogance, and acting gently, which combats rudeness. If you are really in love,

---

[1] https://en.oxforddictionaries.com/definition/arrogant.
[2] http://www.dictionary.com/browse/rude.

you must make authenticity and gentleness two of your chief aims.

4. Love does not insist on its own way.

If you aren't ready to live a selfless life, you aren't ready to pledge your love to someone. When it comes to love and marriage, you cannot succeed if you do not place the needs of your spouse before your own.

If you can't imagine serving the person you are dating, bite your tongue; you aren't ready to even utter this four letter word. If you choose love, you are choosing to make someone else's success your highest goal. Until you can make this type of commitment, you are not in love.

5. Love is not irritable or resentful.

When it comes to relationships, these two enemies are sadly far too common. Life can be demanding and stressful at times. How do you handle stress? Who do you take it out on?

Sadly, we tend to cherish the least those who matter the most. This often results in our significant other bearing the brunt of our irritability which leads to resentment.

Love is when you intentionally choose to live as a team. If you choose to love, you are choosing to fight the two enemies called irritability and resentment. You are on this journey together.

6. Love does not rejoice at wrongdoing but rejoices with the truth.

The key word here is "rejoice." If you both make wrongdoings or failures your focus or harp on each other's inadequacies, your relationship is headed for a catastrophe.

When you choose love, you are choosing to establish a culture in your relationship that celebrates truth. This doesn't mean you ignore weakness or failure; it just means that while you are working to improve in any particular area of weakness, you remain focused on what is true. Paul said in Philippians 4:8:

> *"Finally, brethren, whatever things are true, whatever things are noble, whatever things are just, whatever things are pure, whatever things are lovely, whatever things are of good report, if there is any virtue and if there is anything praiseworthy—meditate on these things."*
>
> (NKJV)

When it comes to love, you must make a conscious choice to celebrate what is true rather than focusing on what is wrong.

7. **Love bears all things, believes all things, hopes all things, endures all things.**

   Everyone blows it at some point, in one way or another. If you have not chosen love, someone's failure will typically drive you away. You'll attempt to avoid getting involved in the situation.

   However, when you have chosen love, the exact opposite is true. You see their weakness and failure as your very own. You'll fight their problems with as much tenacity as your own. Love doesn't point the finger; it helps bear the load.

   How do you know if you are in love? Ask yourself these four questions:

   - *Can I bear the problems of the person I like as if they were my own?*

   - *Can I believe the best about them even if they are exhibiting their worst?*

   - *Can I inspire hope in them if we were to face a hopeless situation?*

   Finally, . . .

   - *Can I endure all things for the sake of our relationship?*

If you choose love, you are choosing to count the cost and pay the price of bearing all things, believing all things, hoping all things and enduring all things for the furtherance of the one you've chosen.

8. **Love never ends.**

   Finally, love is when each person is willing to commit their life to the success of the other through life's triumphs and tragedies. When you tell someone you love them, as it relates to marriage, you are telling them that you are committed to their good—with no strings attached—forever.

Hopefully, this puts the severity of love in a sober perspective.

In the New Testament, there are a few different Greek words used for the word "love." The two primary ones are *phileō* and *agapē*.

Phileō refers to the love of a companion, loving them because they bring you delight and pleasure of some sort.

Agapē, however, refers to the love you have for someone, not out of response to them but because you made a quality, unwavering choice. It is an unconditional love that continues on, even when no love is given in response.

In Ephesians 5, husbands are instructed to *agapē* their wives as Christ loved the Church. You are not in love until you are able to extend love even if nothing is given in response.

We hope that as you have read through each of these eight keys, you have realized how serious love is. It's more than a fleeting emotion. The value of this sacred choice is unparalleled to any other. When the time comes that you find the person you are willing to make this level of commitment to, we pray you would cherish that relationship only second to your relationship with God.

HOW DO I KNOW IF I'M READY FOR MARRIAGE?

Have you found the person you want to spend the rest of your life with? Ready to tie the knot? That's great! Marriage is awesome, but it's probably not what you have in mind. It's not just sex; it's not just romance. Marriage is sharing every aspect of your life with another individual. Don't read this the wrong way. We believe in marriage! Hey, we believe in it so much that, for us, it only comes second to our commitment to Jesus. It's a big deal, but it's not always a bed of roses.

That's why you must ask this question soberly and honestly. We want to help you know with certainty whether or not you are ready for this.

Here are three things to consider about marriage when determining whether or not you are ready to say "I do":

1. **Marriage is not temporary.**

   You are not signing a short-term commitment. The bond of holy matrimony is meant to last as long as you do. While you are both alive, your commitment remains. The vows that are made at the sacred altar of marriage are not weak, nor are they fragile. They cannot be easily broken.

   Until you reach a place of certainty, knowing that you cannot reverse your commitment, you are not ready for marriage. Our pastors often quote Malachi 2:16, when taking couples through pre-marital counseling, reminding them that God said He hates divorce.

   If you come from a home where your parents have separated, you, all the more, have to decide that divorce is not an option. While we were going through pre-marital counseling, we were challenged to make a commitment to eliminate the word "divorce" from our vocabulary when communicating with one another. We don't even use the word in a joking or sarcastic manner. When telling others about the commitment we've made, we've been told on several occasions that we're being a bit extreme.

   You can't afford to be casual towards this commitment. Until you understand how extreme this "until death do us part" decision is, you aren't ready for marriage.

2. Marriage is not cheap.

Despite what the old country song says, you cannot live on love. No, you are going to need some groceries . . . and electricity . . . and some water. Oh, I almost forgot. You're probably going to need a vehicle, as well. By the way, that vehicle won't run without fuel, so you'll need some gas, too. Unlike being single, all your daily living expenses double.

Marriage is expensive!

There will be seasons in your marriage that seem like you have to spend money every time you turn around. This means that prior to marriage, you must determine that you are financially compatible:

- *Who is best at making a budget?*
- *Can you both agree on how to distribute your income?*
- *Do you trust the spending habits of the person you want to marry?*
- *How do you handle your personal finances now?*
- *Do you have a spending problem?* (If you can't control your money now,

while you are single, you are not ready for marriage.)

Though uncomfortable, these questions are essential to starting off on the right foot.

If you really believe you've found the person you want to spend the rest of your life with, we highly recommend you consider the costs of living within marriage. Make a budget, and see if you have the finances to sustain your future household. If your expenditures are more than your combined resources, you're not ready for marriage.

3. Marriage is not always glamorous.

Actually, it's rarely glamorous. Ladies, you need to know that "happy weight" is real! The abs he has right now might not be there a few weeks after you say, "I do." Guys, just a heads up; she doesn't wake up with her make-up fixed and her hair in place.

Sometimes your home will be messy. The trash will be overflowing and the dishes piling up, yet you've made a commitment—and that commitment is meant to stand through the good and the bad.

You don't have to resent the idea of less-than-glamorous moments; you just have to consider the reality that not every moment of your life and coming marriage is going to look like a scene from a Hollywood movie—and that's ok!

Love is when you see your spouse at their worst, and you are still willing to give them your best. Until you can make that kind of commitment, you are not ready for marriage.

Have we talked you out of saying, "I do," yet? We know these aren't the most fun topics to discuss when considering marriage. They can seem like a real damper on the idea of marital bliss, but we can say this from experience: It's better to address them now than wait until after you've made a lifelong commitment.

Though it was uncomfortable at the time, words can't express how thankful we are that someone told us about the "not-so-pleasant" side of marriage.

When you're ready, you will be willing to fully embrace the good and the . . . well, let's just say not-so-good parts of this holy union called marriage.

PART II

THE RULES OF
SEX & PURITY

31

WHAT EXACTLY IS SEX?

Sex has been wrongly defined. The world is at war with this generation's perception of what intimacy really looks like. Is Hollywood right? Is sex a steamy one-night-stand with no real consequences? Maybe sex is just a physical activity: you hook up with whoever you find attractive and fulfill your desires.

While individuals seem more and more prone to model their lives and sexuality after the latest hit tv shows, we've found a better way. Though many in the Church want to shy away from dealing with the subject of sexuality, the Bible fearlessly and relentlessly gives clear direction on the matter.

In 1 Corinthians 6:15-17 (NKJV), the apostle Paul wrote:

"Do you not know that your bodies are members of Christ? Shall I then take the members of Christ and make them members of a harlot? Certainly not! Or

do you not know that he who is joined to a harlot is one body with her? For the two,' He says, *'shall become one flesh. But he who is joined to the Lord is one spirit with Him."*

If we want to see a generation embrace biblical purity, we must boldly stand behind biblical principles. Here are the four ways we define sex:

1. **Sex is a spiritual matter.**

    We cannot ignore the Scripture's spiritual emphasis on sex. Biblically, sex changes the way God, who is Spirit, looks at us. That's one reason that sex is no small issue in His eyes. The good news is: Even if you've completely blown it in this area, we serve the God of restoration. His redemptive power is strong enough to free you from any past mistakes.

2. **Sex is a physical matter.**

    This one shouldn't be too hard to understand. The old saying is true: "It takes two to tango!" For most people, the physical aspect is the most enticing part of the experience. But, sex is not a mere physical act. There is far more to it.

    Even the physical experience is a sacred moment which is why we were never meant to approach it casually. We were not meant to share this experience with just anybody at any time. It was meant to be shared between one man and one woman within the bonds of marriage. Sex is sacred to God, so it should be sacred to us.

3. **Sex is an emotional matter.**

   Unfortunately, many have figured this out as a devastating afterthought. We've heard ample stories of individuals who got caught up in the moment, gave themselves away, and then found their lives in an emotional wreck shortly after.

   Why? Because what you do lasts far beyond the moment you do it. Sex doesn't just make you vulnerable physically, but emotionally, as well. When someone has physical access to our bodies, they also have access to our emotions. This, yet again, proves why sex was never meant to happen outside of marriage. You must guard yourself and make purity a chief aim in your life.

4. **Sex is a binding matter.**

   For married couples, the bond that is formed through sex is remarkable. You truly share something with your spouse that is shared with no one else. While this bond is profound inside of marriage, it is devastating outside of marriage.

Let's say you're reading this and you've messed up sexually. You gave yourself to someone outside of marriage but later surrendered to God. You repented and asked for forgiveness, yet for some reason, you can't escape the guilt of your past. You re-live the mistakes you've made in your mind over and over, even though you've genuinely repented.

The reason for this is simply because, though God has forgiven you, the binding effects of sex outside of marriage are still attached to your life. For full deliverance from the pain and control of your past, we highly recommend that you seek help from your pastor or a trusted spiritual leader. You are not without hope, and God wants you to walk in complete freedom!

We challenge you to go back to the Bible. Open it up, and see what it says. If you do not embrace God's definition of sexuality and purity, you will fall prey to the world's definition.

Be proactive. Be intentional.

Let's start a revolution in the realm of purity!

32

HOW FAR IS TOO FAR?

When it comes to dating, sex, and purity, this is one of the most prominent questions we have been asked.

We can distinctly remember a time in our early dating years when we were at a youth gathering and the topic that evening was sexual purity. At the end, they opened it up for questions, and a kid just a couple of rows in front of us asked, "How far is too far?"

In response, the guy leading the discussion humiliated the kid, making him feel like he was dirty for even having that kind of thought. There was one major problem for us: We were thinking the same thing; we just hadn't asked it.

"Are we allowed to hold hands? Can we kiss? If we can kiss, what kind of kissing?" Ever had those thoughts? Yeah, us, too. Over the past several years, we have come to the conclusion that if you are asking, "How far is too far," you are not dirty; you are normal!

We've all asked that question!

But, what if it's the wrong question?

What if you can find a way to make the most of your relationship and still stay pure? If that's your goal, we have three better questions than, "How far is too far," that you should ask:

1. Does this please God?

> *"And whatever you do, do it heartily, as to the Lord..."*
>
> Colossians 3:23a (NKJV)

Dating has had a bad rap for far too long. There is a way to date that is actually honorable to God.

Next time you start to ask, "How far is too far?" instead ask, "Is this pleasing to God?" This question will help unravel any intentions you may have that aren't aiming for purity.

Remember, God loves you and has your best interests in mind. You don't have to be afraid of asking this question. He is not looking to kill the excitement. He wants you to achieve a healthy place in dating that is both vibrant and pure.

2. **Will I have to hide what I'm doing from anyone?**

   "For nothing is secret that will not be revealed, nor anything hidden that will not be known and come to light."

   Luke 8:17 (NKJV)

   If what you and your date want to do has to be hidden, then it should not be done. While you will probably never feel comfortable parading your affection in front of either of your parents, if push comes to shove, you want to be able to say with confidence that you have nothing to hide.

   Ultimately, as stated in Luke 8, there is nothing you have hidden that will not eventually be brought into the light anyways. Make it one of your highest goals, especially in dating, to live with nothing hidden.

3. **Would I ever encourage someone else to do it?**

   "But whoever causes one of these little ones who believe in Me to stumble, it would be better for him if a millstone were hung around his neck, and he were thrown into the sea."

   Mark 9:42 (NKJV)

Pause for a minute. Think of someone you know who is single, whom you deeply care about. (It may be a sibling or your closest friend.) Now, pretend you are encouraging them to do with someone else what you want to do with your date. Are you giving them good advice? Are you, as a believer, pushing them away from Christ? It's interesting how differently we see things when the tables are turned. If you would not advise someone else to do what you are contemplating, don't do it.

As we wrap up, we want to leave you with a final thought. There is a reason we are so passionate about your sexual purity. When you reserve yourself for marriage, you are able to give yourself to your spouse on your wedding night without anything missing or broken. The more you save, the more you have to offer in that special moment. Even if you've gone further than you would ever like to admit, you can turn to Jesus who is able to bring about complete and total restoration.

We challenge you to take these three questions to heart, and let them guide you on your journey of purity.

33

WHAT SHOULD I DO IF I'VE ALREADY GONE TOO FAR?

Many people find themselves stuck, feeling hopeless, simply because of one bad decision. We do not want to make light of sexual sin. It is no small matter. However, if you have gone too far, you are not out of God's reach. There is still hope!

If you want to live free from your past, here are four things you must do:

1. **You must repent.**

   > *"Now repent of your sins and turn to God, so that your sins may be wiped away."*
   >
   > Acts 3:19 (NLT)

   Before you make another move, you must take this step. While our society is moving further and further away from the call of repentance, heaven isn't.

If you want to get back on track, live free of your failure, and become everything God desires for you to become, this part of the process isn't optional; it is required. Grace is not God ignoring your weakness. Grace is God's power working in your weakness. You are not alone. Acknowledge your sin before God, and lay it on the altar.

2. **You must understand that nothing is beyond repair.**

> *"If we confess our sins, He is faithful and just to forgive us our sins and to cleanse us from all unrighteousness."*
>
> 1 John 1:9 (NKJV)

Oftentimes, we allow the guilt of failure to lead us to a place of condemnation. We start thinking that our failure is so bad that we have absolutely no hope.

Why do we respond to our shortcomings like this?

We respond this way because we've listened to our enemy. Once Satan has convinced you that sin, especially sexual sin, is "not that bad" and you give in, within moments of your compromise, you'll then hear him whisper, "Now you've gone too far! There's nothing you can do to make things right!"

But, the devil is a liar!

Listen, if you have breath in your lungs and a beat in your heart, then you have hope. With Jesus, nothing is beyond repair.

3. You must get help.

> *"Confess your sins to each other and pray for each other..."*
>
> James 5:16a (NLT)

One of the reasons so many Christians live in defeat is because they try to fight the armies of hell all alone. We're convinced the reason most people try to fight alone is because they don't want anyone else to know about their weaknesses.

As long as you try to contain your sin, your sin will contain you. Don't try to fight this by yourself. Find someone you can trust, who will not parade your problems in front of the rest of the world. Then, as soon as you can, have a private meeting and tell them exactly where you are in life and what you are going through. We're not talking about the modified story you wish were true. Uncensored, gut-level honesty is what it takes. Be real, and let them in on where you're at. If freedom is really a priority, then you have to quit hiding in the dark. Expose your failure to a trusted advisor and let them help you step into freedom!

4. **You must let God turn back time.**

> *"'Behold, I will bring the shadow on the sundial, which has gone down with the sun on the sundial of Ahaz, ten degrees backward.' So the sun returned ten degrees on the dial by which it had gone down."*
>
> Isaiah 38:8 (NKJV)

Are you wondering what the sundial of Ahaz and the sun turning back ten degrees has to do with anything? In Hezekiah's time, the sundial of Ahaz was their form of a clock. It's how they kept up with time.

Simply put, God turned back time as a sign to King Hezekiah. What does this mean? If God could turn back time for him, He can turn back time for you. Will He literally cause the earth to go backward in its orbit? We don't know. But, what we do know is that when God washes away your sin, He casts it into the sea, never to be remembered, as though it never happened.

No matter how far you've gone, when you call upon His name in repentance, He can restore everything you have lost, including the things you've lost sexually.

This doesn't mean you shouldn't be honest with your future spouse about your past. It just means that when you tell them about your past, though you wish it had never happened, you can speak freely and confidently that Jesus has redeemed you and has restored all that you have lost. He is the God of restoration!

If you have gone further than you wanted to go and have done more than you wanted to do, the good news is this: Your past does not have to determine your future. Use these four keys to unlock a life of restoration and hope through Jesus, and you will never be the same!

34

DO YOU THINK MY DATE TOLD HIS FRIENDS WE WENT TOO FAR?

We hate to break it to you, but you're probably not going to like our answer. Unfortunately, what you suspect has probably already happened: Yes, he told them.

The sad reality in our culture is that men often treat sex like a trophy. In his eyes, messing around with you made him superior to his friends, and now your sexual escapade has become his bragging rights. So, know this: Whatever you do in private, will, at some point, become public knowledge.

When we first started dating, we had a mutual friend who ended up in a bad relationship. He had a history of sexual promiscuity and really had no business getting back into the dating scene. Nonetheless, he refused to heed anyone's advice and got into a relationship anyways.

We watched this guy's life spiral out of control within just a few short months. First, he tried to hide what he and his girlfriend were doing. Then, he pretended like they were setting boundaries. Finally, he reached a place where he would publicly brag, especially around the guys, about being the first person to get her in bed.

Listen, our friend was a church kid. He had good church leaders and had multiple people confront him multiple times.

Just because you think your date has a halo and wings doesn't mean this can't happen to you. If you mess around, you run the risk of others finding out about your private affairs.

LADIES, HERE'S OUR ADVICE:

If you are in a relationship with a guy who is willing to tarnish your purity, call it off. You are too valuable!

We know how challenging the struggle to remain sexually pure can be, especially in a heated moment. But, you will never give in to temptation and then think to yourself, "I really hope everyone finds out what I did and starts looking at me differently."

If you don't want your name to be tainted by sexual sin, there is only one solution: Reserve sex for marriage. Otherwise, if you choose to be sexually active before marriage, there is a high probability that your man will tell all of his friends—in great detail—all about what the two of you have been up to.

GUYS, A WORD FOR YOU:

If you are the kind of guy that would make a lady have to ask if you've told your friends, you are not a man yet. You're still a child, and you need to grow up before you try to enter the dating world.

There are two things every real man has in common: First, real men value women too much to take their purity from them; and second, real men value their own name and reputation too much to ruin it with sexual sin. You may think it strengthens your public status to brag about your sexual immaturity now, but you will one day regret that your name was ever associated with such a lewd lifestyle.

Grow up, be a man, and value purity.

Sexual sin has a history of making private affairs a public matter. If you don't want people to question your integrity, when it comes to sexuality, remain adamant about choosing purity—even if it costs you a relationship.

Sexual temptation is certain to come in dating, but when your date indicates that they are okay with compromising their standards and indulging in their desires, be bold enough to pull the plug and turn the other way. You are worth more than the cheap thrill that comes from a moment of compromise. Uphold your name and reputation, making purity your highest aim.

35

IS IT OK TO DATE SOMEONE WHO ISN'T A VIRGIN?

Virginity is no small matter. Your sexual status entering into marriage is a big deal. That's why we believe this question is so important. Sadly, more and more people are not reserving sex for marriage.

However, that doesn't mean that those who gave their virginity away before marriage are bad people. We know countless people who were not saved or didn't have a real walk with the Lord who had sex outside of marriage. Sure, they had obstacles to overcome; but when they surrendered their life to Jesus, He made them new.

Here are four questions you must ask when considering whether or not you should date someone who is not a virgin:

1. **Have they repented of their past mistakes?**

    When you found out that the person you are interested in dating wasn't a virgin, did they talk about it casually as if it were insignificant?

When true repentance takes place, there is a somberness about where you once were. Many seem to recount their previous lifestyle of immorality as though they enjoyed it more than life in Jesus. We believe *this*, most often, is simply an indicator that true repentance has not taken place.

As believers, we are not depressed because we were once sinners; we've been made alive in Christ, and we rejoice! However, that doesn't mean we think lightly of our previous life in sin. If you do not see any sense of severity in the person you are considering when they discuss their past, turn away; they aren't a good idea.

2. Do they have any connection with the people they were previously sexually involved with?

This is huge. The connection that is forged during sex is lifelong. Something transpires that you cannot mentally or emotionally erase.

If the person you are considering has a connection with any person they were once sexually involved with, you're in risky territory. We don't advise getting involved in such a situation. The one exception to this rule is if their past sexual history led to a child being born. If the person you are interested in had a baby from a former relationship and you are really interested in them, you must take into consideration the inevitable connection that will exist for the sake of the child. Otherwise, avoid dating anyone who is still closely connected with people they were once sexually involved with.

3. **Have they established accountability in their life that will prevent them from repeating their past?**

When you choose to date someone who has already had sex, you must make sure that there is some type of accountability in place. Otherwise, you could find yourself in the same position as them. The best way to find out how much of a priority purity is for them now is by asking a few pointed questions, such as:

- *"Who are you accountable to?"*

- *"How often do you meet?"*

- *"Does anyone have access to your private messages, Internet, and online history?"*

Questions such as these can reveal the true intent of the heart and help keep you out of a situation that could lead you down a very difficult road of impurity. We've often said that if someone does not value their purity, they will not value yours either.

4. Can you be at peace knowing their past?

The last thing you must be willing to address is how you feel about the life this person once lived. Can you separate them now from what they were then? Will you always have a lingering thought in the back of your mind about their previous sexual encounters?

For a relationship of this nature to be strong and vibrant, you cannot live with these questions. This isn't to say it will never cross your mind, but you cannot allow yourself to dwell on it—ever. If you can't get past knowing what they have done, it doesn't mean you are bad; it just means you're not the one for them. If you can, and the other areas are intact, go for it!

People who have turned to God after giving themselves away before marriage are not damaged goods. They are not subpar or second-class people because of their past mistakes. When they came to God in repentance and allowed Him to restore them, they were washed clean of their past mistakes. If you can see that they now value purity and are genuinely living to please the Lord, then see them the way He does—forgiven, redeemed, and restored!

36

SHOULD I TELL MY DATE ABOUT MY STD?

It is crucial that you build every relationship you have on the foundation of integrity and honesty. This is especially true when it comes to dating. However, there may be parts of your story that you do not feel comfortable sharing—and that's ok... at least at first.

Statistics suggest that one in four Americans will get a sexually transmitted disease (STD) in their lifetime.[1] If you happen to be one of these one-in-four people, there are some serious safety precautions you must be willing to take.

The first and primary precaution is that you talk to your significant other. There are two extremes you want to avoid. The first is telling the wrong person too soon. While you want to be honest in every relationship, if you tell your

---

[1] http://www.hivplusmag.com/prevention/2015/09/25/shocking-stats-stds-america?pg=3#article-content.

date of two weeks about your STD and two weeks later you guys have an argument that leads to a bad break up, your secret could go viral.

The second extreme you want to avoid is waiting too late to talk to them. If you wait until you're about to pop the question, this could lead the person you've been dating to believe that part of your relationship has been a lie—and rightfully so. You do not want to make someone you really care about believe that you've been hiding something from them, especially if they are your potential spouse. Timing, in this case, really is everything.

So, to answer the question: Yes, you must tell them.

But, neither rush into it nor drag your feet. While there is always a risk that they could tell others, regardless how long you wait; you do want to establish a firm foundation of trust before you share your secret.

When the timing is right, here are the three things you need to explain to them:

1. **Explain your past.**

    As a follower of Christ, you've been set free from the bondage of yesterday's mistakes. While it is true that in Jesus you are a new creation, this doesn't mean you can deny what has already happened. To you, it may be "water under the bridge," but it did take place, nonetheless.

If you are at the age where marriage is really an option and you think you may be dating the person who will one day become your spouse, then you need to talk to them about your past. Again, wait until a strong foundation of trust has been built, and then you need to have an honest conversation with them about how far you've gone and why they can trust that you are different now.

Once you have put the ball in their court, it is their choice as to whether or not they'll move forward with you or cut things off. This will, no doubt, be uncomfortable; but it must be done.

2. **Explain your prognosis.**

So, you got more than you bargained for. Unfortunately, even though you've repented, you are carrying the result of a poor decision into your future. Are things getting serious in your relationship? If so, you have to explain your prognosis.

They need to know the condition of your health and how it could potentially affect them. Given that many STDs are highly contagious, this is another conversation that cannot be avoided. If you genuinely care about the person you are with, they need to know the cold, hard facts about what they are getting into.

Fair warning: This could be a deal-breaker for some people. Should your date tell you that your physical condition is too much for them to handle, you must respect their wishes and allow them to go their separate way. Bad decisions have bad consequences; nonetheless, you have to have integrity and make a commitment to do the right thing—even if it costs you.

3. **Explain your plan.**

Welcome to the final phase. Once you have explained what risks are involved, you need to discuss what safety precautions can be taken to protect them. You also need to explain what steps you are taking to achieve better health amidst your illness.

To do this, you need to consult your local physician. Do not even try to strategize or find a solution by reading an article you found online. (The only thing you should be searching for on the Internet, regarding this matter, is which doctor has the best reviews!) With the help of a professional, you can devise a plan that not only puts you on the path of recovery but also ensures their safety. Plus, taking this extra step will let them know you are serious about doing whatever it takes to make sure they are safe. If they are a potential spouse, they need to know that you are concerned about them first and foremost.

You do not want to jeopardize someone else's physical well-being. If your date chooses to stay committed to the relationship, then one day they will look back with much gratitude that you chose to take such extreme precautions to ensure their safety.

If you made a mistake that led to you contracting an STD, there is hope. You do not have to look towards your future with dismay. As a believer, you can trust that your past is behind you, and that God can make all things work together for your good, as He promised in His Word. (See Romans 8:28.)

We challenge you to not let forgiveness be the end. The same God who healed you spiritually can heal you physically. Call upon the name of Jesus, and ask Him to heal your body. Find scriptures about divine health and healing to stand on as you trust God for a breakthrough in your health!

37

WHAT IS SAFE SEX?

Everyone has an opinion about sex. Sadly though, these opinions are becoming more and more influenced by society. This is a major problem because most often the only part of the story that gets told is the glamorous part.

Have you ever heard the old proverb, "A half-truth is a whole lie?" You need to know that those promoting "safe sex" outside of marriage are only telling you a half-truth. Is sex fun? Is it exciting? Is it intense? Yes, but that's not all it is.

The truth is, sex outside marriage is also risky business.

Anytime we talk about the risks of sex outside marriage, someone always thinks that they have an ingenious method that will keep them safe; i.e., wearing two condoms, making an early exit, peeing immediately after sex, etc. You name it; we've probably heard it. Unfortunately for them, these strategies have failed time and time again. Even for the companies that claim that their products are between

99.9% and 100% effective, there's one major detail they often leave out of the equation: Their product is only 99.9% effective if you use it 100% correctly!

If you are attempting to try "safe sex" outside of marriage, there are two major risks you must consider:

1. **Pregnancy.**

    Fox News reported that between 2% and 8% of women get pregnant while on the birth control pill every year.[1] And if you're one who thinks, "Oh, that would never happen to me," think again! It's those who thought this same thing, that make up this percentage.

    There are many variables when it comes to failed birth control methods. That means, if you are sexually active, you are at risk. Children are a gift from God, yet the truth remains: Raising a child is a lot of work! It's not a nine-month commitment; it's a lifetime commitment. Are you ready to put your dreams and goals on hold to raise a kid?

    Ladies, if you were to become pregnant, are you certain that you are with someone who wouldn't bailout and leave you to raise that child on your own?

---

[1] http://www.foxnews.com/story/2008/06/16/five-reasons-women-get-pregnant-while-on-pill.html.

Guys, are you man enough to lay everything else aside to take care of your family? We hope you understand that safe sex sometimes leads to the unexpected. Aside from the sin issue, which is the most important factor; if you aren't ready to put your life on hold to raise a child, then you aren't ready to have sex.

2. **Disease.**

Statistics suggest that one in four Americans have a sexually transmitted disease (STD) or infection (STI).[2] While certain contraceptives can help in preventing such diseases and infections from spreading, there is certainly no guarantee that they will work.

In fact, without any genitalia involved, you can still contract an infection or disease by mere skin-to-skin contact. In many cases, when someone contracts an illness from sexual activity, it is unfortunately something they battle for the rest of their lives. It just takes one failed product or mishap to change your entire world.

Is this a risk you really want to take? Do you want to have to talk to your future spouse about a disease you contracted from a past relationship? This possibility is a serious risk factor for anyone who's sexually active. If you aren't going

---

2 http://www.hivplusmag.com/prevention/2015/09/25/shocking-stats-stds-america?pg=3#article-content.

to play by the rules, it's a risk you must be willing to take.

The truth is, there's only one way to have safe sex, and that's inside of marriage. Can things happen that you hadn't planned on in a marriage? You bet, but it's better for it to happen with someone who has committed to spending the rest of their life by your side than with an individual who could be gone the minute you turn around.

Within a biblical union, sex is beautiful. Play by the rules. As tempting as it may be to try to cut some corners here and there, stay within the parameters that God has laid out; they are there for your good. Without risk and worry, reserve sex for the sacred bond that's meant to be shared solely between a husband and a wife.

38

IS ORAL SEX "TECHNICALLY" SEX?

We get it. If you are in a relationship and you find yourself asking what is and is not allowed, we can help you out. We've been there.

When you find someone you really like, there is a push to get everything you can out of the relationship. But, if you are not careful, this can end up costing you—big time!

Typically, in regards to sex, when people start getting "technical" about things, that's when they get into trouble. Are you getting "technical" about things in your relationship? If you are asking questions like, "Is oral sex 'technically' considered sex?" or, "Is it 'technically' sex if we just use our hands?" then you are heading down the wrong path.

God is not intimidated by your questions, and there's nothing wrong with wanting to know what is allowed and what is not; however, to go in the right direction, you need to ask the right questions. So, if you're asking if something is "technically" sex, then you are asking the wrong thing.

Rather than asking if it is "technically" considered sex, ask if it is considered sin. Now, how do you determine what is and is not considered sin?

Here are three ways to determine what is and is not considered sin:

1. **The Word.**

    > *"God means what he says. What he says goes. His powerful Word is sharp as a surgeon's scalpel, cutting through everything, whether doubt or defense, laying us open to listen and obey. Nothing and no one is impervious to God's Word. We can't get away from it—no matter what."*
    >
    > Hebrews 4:12-13 (MSG)

    Sin is a spiritual issue that can be easily over spiritualized. Here's what we mean. When it comes to knowing God's will, we have a tendency to do some bizarre things. How many times, have you asked for a sign from heaven when you were unsure of God's will about something—without ever even looking to see what the Bible had to say about it? Do we really have to ask God to perform a stunt every time we are unsure about something? Does He have to speak audibly with a host of angels surrounding us, singing in harmonious glory for us to know His will? The answer is, "No."

Will there be things we face in life that the Bible doesn't give a black and white answer to? Sure. However, that's rare. If there's a situation that you do not know right from wrong, explore God's Word on the matter. When you search the Bible, the Bible searches you. Then, you can discover with clarity what is and is not sin.

2. The Holy Spirit

> *"Nevertheless I tell you the truth. It is to your advantage that I go away; for if I do not go away, the Helper will not come to you; but if I depart, I will send Him to you. And when He has come, He will convict the world of sin . . ."*
>
> John 16:7-8a (NKJV)

In this verse, Jesus tells us the Holy Spirit is our Helper, and one of His primary jobs is to show us right from wrong, what is and is not sin.

Once you were born again and surrendered your life to Jesus, did you notice how some of the things you once had no problem participating in all of a sudden started making you uneasy?

That's the Holy Spirit.

Though uncomfortable, that gnawing feeling you get in the pit of your stomach isn't just hunger pangs; it's a gift! It's God's way of letting you know something is wrong.

If you find yourself in a situation, where sexual temptation is escalating, and you aren't in a position to whip out a Bible to see if you are heading in the wrong direction, just listen to the Holy Spirit.

There may even be moments, such as there were for us, where you would love to go a certain way, but you just know the Holy Spirit is waving a warning flag. Follow Him, and resist your flesh. If the Spirit of God lives in you, He will not let you remain comfortable with sin.

3. Spiritual authority.

> *"Obey your spiritual leaders, and do what they say. Their work is to watch over your souls, and they are accountable to God."*
>
> Hebrews 13:17a (NLT)

This final point may be the most challenging of all. In and of ourselves, none of us enjoy being told what to do, and yet the Word says:

"Without guidance, people fall..."

Proverbs 11:14a (HCSB)

We cannot over emphasize that in our endeavor to stay pure, we found that few things have the value of spiritual leaders. You need someone who will not only ask you tough questions but someone who you can turn to without embarrassment when you have tough questions to ask.

There is no better place to find these spiritual leaders than in your local church. We are forever indebted to the leaders whom we were able to turn to in privacy and confidence with questions just like the ones you are asking. Do whatever it takes to find these kind of leaders. Then, when you find them, submit to them, and follow their instruction. It may be frustrating at times now, but you will be thankful later that you chose this path.

Time and time again, as we have talked about *The Rules of Romance Before Marriage* with this generation, we've said one simple truth: On your wedding night, you will not look back wishing you had given more of your body to your ex.

When it comes to oral sex, you can know—plain and simple—it's sin. If Jesus considered it sin to look at someone with lust, how much more when you participate in sexual actions?

Don't waste your time looking for what is "technically" right and "technically" wrong. Instead, live by a higher standard. Go above and beyond. If you will honor God with your purity, He will honor your relationship with His presence—and there is no greater reward than that.

39

WHAT KIND OF KISSING IS APPROPRIATE?

Can we be honest with you? We don't want just everyone knowing this, so we need you to keep it a secret. You promise our secret is safe with you? Alright, here goes. We didn't do so well in this area when we started dating. We kissed at the wrong places, at the wrong times. It was only by the grace of God and the fear of our parents that we never moved past a sloppy wet kiss into something far more risqué. We certainly did not do this one "appropriately."

Our hope is that, through this chapter, we can share truths that will help you avoid the mistakes we made. We do not believe that you have to follow the crowd's example of romantic dating. Who said you have to kiss within your first few dates? As a matter of fact, who said you even have to kiss at all while you are dating? Don't settle for a mediocre standard.

We have some friends, Mark and Kaylee Alicea, from the Bronx, New York, who completely redefined the norm. This may be shocking to you, but they actually waited until marriage to kiss! How amazing is that? We believe their testimony is proof that you, too can achieve the impossible.

You could carry the story we wish we were able to carry. Are you up for a challenge? There are three factors to take into account when determining whether or not to kiss before marriage:

1. **Risk.**

    "Run from anything that stimulates youthful lusts."

    2 Timothy 2:22 (NLT)

    For us, personally, kissing was never a good idea while dating. Is it sin? No, but it is dangerous, and it can turn for the worse really quickly. Kissing is risky business.

    We took time to ask Mark and Kaylee a few questions, and their response as to why they decided not to kiss could not prove this point any better. They said, "We realized early on that kissing could easily lead to real trouble." If the thought of kissing your date *"stimulates youthful lust,"* the risk of where that could lead should be enough to make you truly consider making this courageous commitment.

2. **Reality.**

> *"Be sober-minded; be watchful. Your adversary the devil prowls around like a roaring lion, seeking someone to devour."*
>
> 1 Peter 5:8 (ESV)

We understand that hearing of a couple who waited until marriage to kiss can be inspiring—and it should be! Yet, we have discovered that when we make decisions based upon inspiration alone, we tend to walk right into a trap. Once the tingling feeling is gone and their story doesn't sound as compelling, will you still have what it takes to fulfill your commitment and stick it out?

Here's our advice: Don't make this kind of decision while you are floating on cloud nine. Wait until reality has kicked back in. If you are dating, you really need to discuss it and pray about it with your date. Then, both of you need to come to a sober, realistic, mutual agreement that you can each stay faithful to. Otherwise, you are a making a commitment that you will not be able to uphold.

3. **Reward.**

> *"The wicked earns deceptive wages, but one who sows righteousness gets a sure reward."*
>
> Proverbs 11:18 (ESV)

This is probably the biggest regret we have when looking back over our early years of dating. We wish we would have sown more into what was right rather than what was merely enjoyable. All of this really made sense after our wedding night. There was something so special about having reserved sex for just each other inside of marriage. It was so significant to us that without a doubt if we had a "do-over," we would even go to the extreme of waiting to share our first kiss at the altar on our wedding day. We asked Mark and Kaylee if they have ever regretted their decision to wait until marriage to kiss, and they said, "Absolutely not! At the altar on our wedding day, we discovered that it was well worth it!"

While you are dating, there will, undoubtedly, be frustrating moments that you face if you make this commitment. But, we are thoroughly convinced it would be, as the Alicea's said—"Well worth it!"

If you are like us and have not waited until marriage to kiss, we want to leave you with two final thoughts. First, do not condemn yourself. We are not by any means saying you are sinful or less valuable because of what you have done.

Lastly, it's not too late. Even if you are in a relationship with someone and you have already kissed, you can still make a change and start this commitment together from here out going forward. We know this will be challenging. No one is suggesting it will be easy; but when your wedding day comes around, you will be glad you chose to wait.

Are you in?

Go for it!

40

HOW MUCH PDA IS TOO MUCH?

Public display of affection (a.k.a., PDA)—where should we begin? First, you should know, we're not against it. If you're with someone who you are actually serious about, then PDA is fine—in moderation; that's the key.

Here are seven rules of romance for all of your public displays of affection:

1. **Are you making your date uncomfortable?**

    We get it. You are in love, and you want the entire world to know. But before you take your courageous stand publicly, ask yourself, "How would this make my date feel?" Look, we have all seen a relationship where the guy's feelings are much deeper than the girl's feelings or vice versa. In this kind of relationship, PDA can become very uncomfortable, very quickly.

Any type of affection shown publicly sends a message. Though you may not be all that into your date, once your friends catch you holding hands, they are likely to think something much different.

If all of the sappy affection your date shows you in public makes you feel uneasy, then let them know. Set boundaries! Be clear on what is and is not ok with your date.

RULE #1

IF IT MAKES THEM UNCOMFORTABLE, IT'S OFF-LIMITS.

2. **Are you making others blush?**

I'll never forget my first week in high school. I almost went into shock! Coming from a small middle school that strongly upheld their strict policies, I had anticipated the next four years leading up to graduation to be no different. Boy, was I wrong!

There were couples swapping spit in nearly every corner. I could literally feel the blood rushing to my face. No one is interested in seeing you and your date mouth-to-mouth. It can wait. Have a little class.

RULE #2

A RED FACE IS YOUR PDA STOP SIGN. IF YOU SEE ONE, YOU NEED TO STOP DOING WHATEVER YOU'RE DOING.

3. **The parent test.**

    We knew a guy (We'll call him "Tyler.") who, in the world of PDA, epitomized everything you should never be. To this day, when this guy comes to mind, the only way we can see him is with his face glued to another one of his girlfriends'.

    We are writing about PDA to try to prevent you from ever becoming like Tyler.

    He'd been talked to by countless people about how inappropriate his actions were, but nothing seemed to work. Finally, his dad came up with a brilliant idea.

    One weekend when Tyler had gone to the mall with all his friends, his parents decided to show up. When they spotted he and his friends in the food court, they got within viewing distance, and then tested their idea. Right there in front of all his friends, they started kissing and hugging up on each other. When Tyler saw his parents, he took off running as fast as he could to stop them, as all of his friends were laughing and making fun of them.

Tyler yelled loud enough to get their attention, but not enough to bring any more attention to them. "Stop! What are you guys doing? You're embarrassing me in front of all my friends!" Tyler had fallen right into his dad's trap. With a sly grin on his face, his dad said, "We're just doing to you what you and your girlfriend keep doing to us."

This marked the end of Tyler's wild PDA adventures. Rule number three is the moral of the story.

RULE #3

IF YOU WOULD BE EMBARRASSED BY YOUR PARENTS DOING IN PUBLIC, WHAT YOU AND YOUR DATE DO IN PUBLIC, THEN DON'T DO IT.

4. **That's not their name, and that's not your voice.**
While pet names and baby talk may be cute to you, it is nauseating to everyone else. PDA is not just what you do, it's also what you say.

While we all know that talking vulgarly is unacceptable, many dismiss the little things that cause others to clam up. If you want to make everyone around you feel awkward, just talk to your date like no one else is in the room. The strange voice, coupled with the weird names you call each other, will certainly turn heads.

Though you should always treat your significant other with the utmost care and respect, you don't have to do it at the expense of public etiquette. At least, while you're around others, use their real name and your real voice. Otherwise, don't go out in public. It's just weird!

RULE #4

REFRAIN FROM USING PET NAMES AND BABY TALK IN PUBLIC.

5. **If it's covered, it's off-limits.**

During high school, we saw our fair share of awkward trends. One in particular was a bit more disturbing than the rest. A lot of guys started walking around with their hand tucked into their girlfriend's back pocket.

Weird, right?

While reminiscing about those obscure times, we came to this conclusion: If you can't see it with your eyes, you shouldn't touch it with your hands. This not only applies when you're in public but private, as well.

So, what should you do, undress? No! There is an area, commonly referred to as "the triangle zone," which is off-limits. This zone is the area covering the chest, the crotch, and the behind. If you follow our fifth rule, you'll stay clear of this area, and stay in safe territory.

RULE #5
DON'T TOUCH WHAT'S COVERED.

6. **The world is still spinning.**

   When it comes to PDA, how much is too much? We have a simple question that we use as a rule of thumb. Ask yourself: "Is my public display of affection stealing the focus of others?" If the answer is, "No," you're fine; if, "Yes," you are out of bounds.

   When PDA becomes a distraction, it becomes a problem. Even though you're in love, the world keeps spinning. People have better things to focus on. Life can't be put on hold just because you're head-over-heels for each other.

   Let's say you and your date are in church. It's a little chilly, so you decided to bust a move.

You do the fake yawn and wrap your arm around your lady. As you do it, you notice that a few people on the other side of the room are now looking at you instead of engaging with the minister. Is your arm being around your date really more important than the life-changing Word of God being planted in someone's heart? No! The sixth rule is simple:

RULE #6

DON'T BE DISTRACTING.

7. **This isn't theater.**

    While attending a high school choir performance, we witnessed a very sad PDA scene. A young lady decided that she was going to make a public declaration of her unending love for her boyfriend, who would be graduating that May. She had it all mapped out in her mind from beginning to end, and it was going to be epic!

    And epic, it was—an epic failure!

    The curtains opened, and the show began. When it came time for her performance, she mustered up the courage and took the stage. Before her act, she gave a super-sappy speech about her boyfriend and dedicated the song she was going to sing, to him. Then, in the middle of her singing performance, she walked off the stage and into the crowd, where she stopped and sang the rest of her song right in front of his face!

Can you guess what happened at the end of her song? Cheering? Chanting?

Nope. Crickets . . . not a sound! An awkward silence fell over the entire theater! Sure, in movies and musicals, this type of PDA is noble. But, in real life? Not so much!

So, is it ok to take such a bold stand? Can you have a moment where you publicly display your affection for your date in a dramatic way? Sure! Just proceed with caution.

Here's all we're saying: You should dream big. Be heroic. Envision your plan with a soundtrack behind it; but when it comes to PDA, it's best to be more conservative. Otherwise, when all is said and done, you might be a little embarrassed if no one is clapping and your date is looking for a table to crawl under and hide.

RULE #7

DREAM BIG, ACT SOBER.

How Much PDA is Too Much?

PDA is a big deal! The way you express your affection in public says a lot about who you are. We want to help you stay in bounds. There is a balance you can find that will allow you to show affection but with discretion and dignity. We believe these prescribed rules can help you stay on the right track and strike the necessary balance!

41

IS IT A SIN TO CHECK SOMEONE OUT?

Have you ever felt the burn? If not, just hold on. It's inevitable. You're going to have to face it at some point. Not just you, but everyone. One day, you will just be sitting there, minding your own business, and in will walk someone you can't ignore. Their look, their frame, their clothes (or the lack of them)—something about them is intriguing. At some point, you will be caught off guard. Everyone experiences this. That's not the problem.

The real problem is not what you see, but rather *how you handle* what you see. How will you respond? Oftentimes, thoughts mingle with desire; and suddenly you have fallen into the trap called "lust." Jesus dealt with the issue of lust sharply in scripture:

> "But I say to you that whoever looks at a woman to lust for her has already committed adultery with her in his heart."
>
> Matthew 5:28 (NKJV)

This truth turned the world on its ear. According to this verse, lust is not simply a matter of action but a matter of thought. Jesus came on the scene and immediately raised the bar. Lust is not about someone catching your attention; it's about them keeping it.

So, can you check someone out without sinning? If you can, it won't be for long. If that's your method, buckle up; you're going to crash. We have a better solution. While most believe our generation is doomed in the realm of purity, we believe differently. As a matter of fact, we believe the exact opposite. We are convinced that this is the generation that will start a revolution in the realm of purity. You don't have to be a victim of temptation. Lust may be your greatest enemy, but it doesn't have to be your lord. We need a paradigm shift.

Here are four truths you must know if you are going to win the war against lust:

TRUTH #1

PEOPLE ARE NOT OBJECTS.

People are more than the skin they wear. Our society is facing a major tragedy, in that everything these days is sexualized. Sex is the leading tool in marketing right now. Think about it. How many TV shows, music videos, and even commercials have you seen that have nothing to do with sexuality? Yet, they are using people in the most provocative ways to promote their products and services. The world's drive in sexualized marketing has led our society to one of its darkest places, where we now primarily see people as objects.

The highlight of any individual is not what you see on the outside; the highlight is what's on the inside.

Newsflash: You are not a product that is up for sale.

Every person has a story and a purpose. Next time you are tempted to indulge in your lustful desires, just remember that the person you are fantasizing over is not some sexual object that exists for your pleasure. You must change your perspective.

TRUTH #2

YOUR THOUGHTS ARE YOUR RESPONSIBILITY.

I was having lunch with a friend one day when a girl in cut-off shorts walked by. As soon as she passed us, I noticed that my friend had dropped his eyes and followed her until she was out of sight. "What are you looking at?" I asked. He was caught red-handed. Embarrassed, he stuttered and fumbled around his words and eventually said, "I couldn't help it. Besides, if she didn't want me to look, she shouldn't have worn that!" He was right in saying she shouldn't have worn that, but he was wrong in saying that he couldn't help himself.

While someone's choice of attire can make temptation all the more difficult, ultimately you are the one in charge of what you do with what you see.

As believers, we have been given a Helper, the Holy Spirit, who can help us extinguish the fires of temptation even in the most challenging situations. So, next time you're facing temptation that seems insurmountable, whisper a simple four-letter word to the Holy Spirit: "HELP!"

TRUTH #3

YOU CANNOT JUSTIFY WHAT GOD CONDEMNS.

A few years ago, we met with someone whose struggle with lust had almost taken over their life. They were hurting and broken and needed some serious help. When we sat down for our meeting, one of the first questions they asked was, "If lust is sin, why does it seem so natural?"

The answer is simple: In a broken world, wrong seems right, and right seems wrong. Sadly, the individual we were meeting with had bought into the idea that because their lust problem was a "struggle," God would excuse it.

There's just one major problem with that philosophy: Your struggle cannot change God's Word. Jesus made it clear—in black and white—that lust is a sin, and He will not change His mind because of someone's struggle. In fact, He has done something better. He has given us grace, the divine power to overcome every temptation we will ever face.

The reality is, without Jesus, we are all just broken people in a broken world, making bad decisions. We hope you see more and more that Jesus is your only hope. If you want to live free from the vice of lust, you must stop trying to justify what God has condemned, and embrace His grace!

TRUTH #4

YOU MUST BE QUICK TO REPENT.

If in your aim for purity you fall short, don't settle for defeat. There is only one thing your enemy loves more than when you commit sin, and that's when you settle in it.

Scripture holds no short list of those who fell into the trap of lust and immorality. So, if you've blown it, you are not alone. Don't let your failure define you.

The Message Bible paraphrase renders Proverbs 24:15-16 powerfully:

> *"Don't interfere with good people's lives; don't try to get the best of them. No matter how many times you trip them up, God-loyal people don't stay down long; soon they're up on their feet, while the wicked end up flat on their faces."*

The only way you can be defeated is if you choose to settle into your failure. Cry out to God, be quick to repent, and get back up.

These truths have the power to transform your life. We are not victims of a carnal appetite. We can live free from the grip of lust and maintain purity even when we feel the burn of temptation all around us.

42

IS IT WRONG TO HAVE FEELINGS FOR THE SAME SEX?

In this day and age, there are a lot of theories surrounding homosexuality. As time goes on, our culture seems to be growing increasingly more open to the idea. Some of the most-watched television shows in America have characters that identify themselves as part of the homosexual community.

Our society has a huge demographic of individuals who celebrate the courage of anyone who publicly "comes out of the closet." While it seems to be growing far more common, it has not always been this way. As a matter of fact, our forefathers would blush at much of what is going on in our nation today.

Is it right? Is it wrong? Can you be a Christian and still be attracted to the same sex? When it comes to same sex attractions, if you are a Christian, there are six things you cannot do:

1. You cannot ignore scripture.

If you place your faith in Jesus as your Savior, you must surrender to Him as Lord. You cannot have one without the other. The primary way you surrender to Him as Lord is by believing and abiding by biblical principles.

The apostle Paul straightforwardly addressed the issue, regarding those who indulged in the practice of homosexuality:

> *"God abandoned them to their shameful desires. Even the women turned against the natural way to have sex and instead indulged in sex with each other. And the men, instead of having normal sexual relations with women, burned with lust for each other. Men did shameful things with other men, and as a result of this sin, they suffered within themselves the penalty they deserved."*
>
> Romans 1:26-27 (NLT)

Clearly, the apostle, as the mouthpiece of God, did not affirm same-sex relations. He reiterated God's displeasure towards homosexuality in other writings, as well. There is no way, from a biblical standpoint, to both follow God and practice a lifestyle of homosexuality.

2. You cannot embrace homosexuality as your identity.

Over and over again, we have heard individuals who struggle with same sex attraction say, "It's who I am." One of the greatest mistakes someone can make in this life is allowing a struggle to define them. Same-sex attractions may be something you struggle with, but it is not who you are; it is not your identity. There is so much more to you than who you find attractive. You are too important to be defined by your hang-ups.

What makes you significant is not what you struggle with; it's who you've surrendered to. As a believer, even in the midst of temptation, the most significant thing about you is that God calls you His child—and that is your identity.

3. You cannot justify sin.

Can you recall, as a little kid, getting caught in the middle of doing something wrong and immediately responding, "Yeah, but they . . . !" as you went on to explain how someone else had done something worse than you?

Have you ever been guilty of that?

Yeah, us, too!

It is the tendency of fallen humanity to automatically bring attention to those who have done worse. As we discovered in Romans 1, we cannot deny that homosexuality is a sin.

Do take note, however, that it is neither the temptation nor the attraction that is sin. The problem comes down to what you yield to and what you act upon. It's at that point when you cross over into sin.

When you stand before God, you will not be able to justify the wrongs you have done by pointing at someone else's failures. Those who have chosen a homosexual lifestyle, in violation of God's Word, will not be able to point to a murderer and say, "Yeah, but what they did was worse." When you have to give an account of your life before God, He will not ask you about what your neighbor did; He will only ask you to answer for what you have done.

4. **You cannot live in condemnation.**

We do not want anyone struggling with same-sex attractions to walk away feeling hopeless after reading this chapter. Furthermore, we certainly don't want to participate in what so many others in the Church have done and make you feel as though you are weird or incompetent. God forbid! The truth is, for both gay and straight, we are all broken without Jesus. The heterosexual couple sleeping together outside of marriage is just as guilty as the homosexual couple sleeping with one another.

While it is our deepest prayer that you would truly sense God's convicting power and seek deliverance, we do not want you to walk in condemnation. There is one primary difference between conviction and condemnation. With condemnation, you're stuck and hopeless; but with conviction, there is hope and freedom. No matter how far you have gone down the road of same-sex relations, there is hope for anyone who calls upon the name of Jesus! (See Romans 10:13.) If you have breath in your lungs, there is hope in Christ for tomorrow!

5. **You cannot win this battle alone.**

As it is for those battling premarital sex, pornography, or any other type of sexual promiscuity, if you really want freedom, you have to get help. Sexual sin has a tendency to linger.

Here's what we mean.

You can repent, genuinely mean it, and promise God that you will never go back and do it again . . . and then find yourself in the exact same position the next week. When sexual sin hooks someone, it hooks them deep. This is why sex was designed to be between one man and one woman inside the bonds of marriage.

If you are fighting a battle with homosexuality, find a trusted leader you can talk to confidentially. And when we say "a leader," we do not mean a friend who will just sympathize with you. No, you need to turn to a leader, preferably a pastor, who will not compromise the Word of God and will commit to walking with you on your road to freedom.

There is no need to publicly broadcast what you are battling. It's no one's business. Tackle this issue under the guidance of no more than two or three key leaders.

6. You cannot win without Jesus.

Beyond anything else you have read thus far in this chapter, you must know that the only way to conquer the enemy you are fighting is by the grace of the Lord Jesus Christ. You cannot do this in your own strength.

The good news is that Jesus loves you so much that He's been willing to fight on your behalf all along. All you have to do is ask. In sincerity and honesty, cry out to God and ask for deliverance. When you place your faith in Jesus, the Bible says:

> "The Spirit of God, who raised Jesus from the dead, lives in you."
>
> Romans 8:11 (NLT)

This means you do not have to depend on your own abilities to win. As a matter of fact, you *can't* win this on your own. But, the same One who defeated the grave wants to help.

With Jesus, you cannot lose!

We want to end by once again saying that you are never too far gone. If you have battled with homosexuality, you have what it takes to win the war. Even if you've been mistreated and made fun of because of this struggle, know that Jesus loves you. Not only does He love you, but He is eager to help you. You do not have to live at the mercy of temptation. You can overcome the powers of darkness.

We hope you will embrace these points and get on the path to true freedom. You can get the victory!

43

HOW DO I BREAK MY ADDICTION TO PORN?

According to the statistics, we are in serious trouble. A survey study of men and women between the ages of 18 to 30 was done by the Barna Group on the subject of pornography.[1] The results it revealed were staggering, making these suggestions:

- 79% of men and 63% of women watch pornography every month.

- 93% of boys and 62% of girls have been exposed to pornography before the age of 18.

According to another study done by Tru Research, over 70% of teens have done something to hide their online behavior from their parents.[2]

Sadly, the list goes on and on.

---

[1] http://www.covenanteyes.com/resources/download-your-copy-of-the-pornography-statistics-pack/.
[2] ibid.

There is one good thing about these statistics: They can only record what has happened in the past; they do not have to determine where we go from here. Now it's up to us to change what they will record in the future.

Here are four proven steps to overcome pornography:

STEP #1
QUIT PRETENDING.

The first step to winning this war is admitting that you are in a battle. Have you ever heard the phrase, "Fake it until you make it?" That motto has one major flaw: People who fake it never make it.

There is one primary reason we try to pretend that everything is okay publicly—you know, putting our best act on, when in actuality, we are on the brink of collapse. That reason?

Shame.

We fear what others would think of us if they knew our failures. Innately, we are all aware that sexual promiscuity is unacceptable. Thus, shame and guilt always show up when we have crossed the line.

When you mess up, you only have two choices: You can either try to hide your mistake, which only makes matters worse; or you can come clean, which is the only real solution.

Here's our advice: Whether you are flirting with the idea of pornography or you find yourself in an all-out war, the only way you can win the battle you are fighting in the dark is by bringing it into the light. Quit fighting this alone. Be bold, be courageous, and get help!

STEP #2
COMMIT TO DAILY DEVOTION.

Everyone faces temptation—and when we say everyone, we mean everyone, with no exceptions. You are not dirty or weird because you have been tempted to do something you know you shouldn't.

Now, listen. We are not here to justify temptation; we want you to know how to handle it. How do you respond when the tempter comes? Temptation is not the issue; how you respond to temptation is the issue. Should you just try to think good thoughts until the bad thoughts go away? Maybe put yourself in solitary confinement without any Internet access?

We've got a better idea—or, actually, the Word does:

> "How can a young man cleanse his way? By taking heed according to Your Word."
>
> Psalms 119:9 (NKJV)

The Bible is the most essential ingredient to a life of purity. You must embrace devotion as a daily ritual. Get in the Word! Meditate on what you're reading. Memorize scripture that you can say out loud whenever you are confronted with temptation.

When Jesus was tempted, He didn't fight the tempter with positive thoughts or even signs and wonders; He fought with the Word: *". . . It is written . . ."* Your Bible is your ticket to victory. You can do this! Get in the Word!

STEP #3
SET UP INTERNET FILTERS.

Setting up an Internet filter is a good practice for every person with access to the Web. The sad reality in our day is that you do not have to look for pornography to see it.

According to a study done by the Kaiser Family Foundation, 70% of teens between the ages of 15 and 17 have stumbled upon pornography online without even looking for it.[3] What does this mean? It means there are people hooked on pornography today just because they were exposed to it without actively looking for it.

---

3 http://www.covenanteyes.com/resources/download-your-copy-of-the-pornography-statistics-pack/.

Struggling or not, an Internet filter is an excellent safety precaution. Look at it as being the guardrails of cyber space with the porn industry driving all over the Internet. With someone like that behind the wheel, an accident is inevitable. However, you do not have to be detoured by someone else's bad decision. There are Internet filters that will block pornography from popping up while you're browsing the Web, which can help keep you out of a ditch. While the ultimate goal is for you to overcome temptation, with or without a filter, why risk putting yourself in harm's way? Set up some guardrails; get an Internet filter.

STEP #4
FIND AN ACCOUNTABILITY PARTNER.

You need someone who will, on a regular basis, ask you pointed questions that no one else will. For example, my pastor asks me regularly, "Caleb, how are you doing with purity?" We have accountability partners in our lives because we have learned that whatever we do not address, we ultimately excuse.

Say you're home alone, scrolling through your smart phone and come across a provocative image. It's enticing and you're weak, so you give in. Once you've come to your senses, what are you going to do? Will you own up to your mistake and establish a credible game plan to avoid repeating the same scenario? Probably not.

What typically happens is, you feel bad about your decisions and then take some time assuring yourself that you will never go there again—and that's about the extent of how most people address their personal weaknesses. They think about it for a moment until they start to feel better. Then, from then on, they do their best to keep their mistakes out of sight and out of mind.

Humans avoid addressing personal weaknesses at all cost. There is a major problem with this reality. Every time you fail to really address the areas that you've fallen short in, you make it that much easier to excuse your moment of weakness in the future.

This is why an accountability partner is invaluable. We all need someone who will confront the problems in our lives that we try to avoid. This is especially true when it comes to pornography. Accountability is an essential part of a life of purity.

We cannot stress these principles enough. Whether you've had a daily struggle with this issue or you have never struggled with it a day in your life, these steps are a proven game plan that will help you achieve a life of integrity and purity. You cannot avoid temptation, but you can overcome it!

44

IS MASTURBATION A SIN?

When we did a brief survey to find the most asked questions surrounding dating and purity, this one was right at the top of the list. At first, this really concerned us but probably for a different reason than what you are thinking.

We were not concerned because the question was being asked; we were concerned because the Church was not answering it. If you have ever thought about whether or not it's wrong to masturbate, you're not alone. You are not dirty or strange. You have a serious question that deserves a serious answer. So, why are ministers not tackling this issue?

After digging a little deeper, we realized that the primary reason the Church is not saying anything about masturbation is because the Bible is not too clear about the subject. That's right. Anyone who says the Bible explicitly condemns the act of masturbation as a sin has to take great liberty to do so. Between the Old and New Testament, there are no direct mentions of masturbation being a sin.

But, hold up a minute.

This doesn't give you a pass to do whatever you want. When it comes to masturbation and whether it's right or wrong, there is one major problem standing in the way: lust. Can you commit an action so closely related to sex without having sexually-provocative thoughts?

In His famous "Sermon on the Mount," Jesus had some very strong words to say about lust. He said:

> "You have heard that it was said to those of old, 'You shall not commit adultery.' But I say to you that whoever looks at a woman to lust for her has already committed adultery with her in his heart."
>
> Matthew 5:27-28 (NKJV)

Pretty intense, right? Well, hold on 'cause He's just getting started. He goes on to say in the following verse:

> "If your right eye causes you to sin, pluck it out and cast it from you; for it is more profitable for you that one of your members perish, than for your whole body to be cast into hell."
>
> Matthew 5:29 (NKJV)

This is why you cannot afford to do anything that would inspire lust, including masturbation. It's quite simple.

Lust leads to sin, and sin leads to hell. In concluding this portion of scripture, Jesus gives one final verse that has been a central piece to the debate on masturbation:

> *"And if your right hand causes you to sin, cut it off and cast it from you; for it is more profitable for you that one of your members perish, than for your whole body to be cast into hell."*
>
> Matthew 5:30 (NKJV)

Many have suggested, since in context this verse is regarding lust, that Jesus could be referring to masturbation. That certainly could be true; however, we think there is something more.

It is our belief that Jesus had one primary point He wanted to get across during this phase of His message. It wasn't self-mutilation or a call to do something physically absurd. There was a reason He was being extreme with His speech. That reason—He wanted you to be extreme about walking in purity. The ultimate takeaway is that He wants you to wage war with anything that could jeopardize your purity. Just a little earlier in verse eight of this same chapter, He said, *"Blessed are the pure in heart, for they shall see God,"* (NKJV). He wants you to walk in purity, so that nothing has the ability to keep you from seeing Him.

Now, we want to challenge you. Rather than asking if masturbation is a sin, why not ask a better question? Why not ask what you've come to know, what Jesus was really concerned about? Ask yourself this: "Does this push me towards purity or away from it?"

Paul had this to say about it:

"Let there be no sexual immorality, impurity, or greed among you. Such sins have no place among God's people."

Ephesians 5:3 (NLT)

You have what it takes, no matter the cost, to live a life of purity. To those in their teens and twenties, especially, you have the extra challenge of battling raging hormones. It's important for you to know this: If you feel like you are in the boxing ring with temptation, this doesn't mean you have done something wrong. It simply means your body is going through a process that heightens your sexual desire. So, don't condemn yourself if an impure thought crosses your mind. Just take that thought captive and make a conscious decision to choose purity. If Christ lives within you, then you have what it takes to win the battle and come out on top.

45

DO I NEED TO REPENT FOR HAVING WET DREAMS?

Guys, we need to talk. Some of you have been trying to hide something. You've felt guilty, confused, and ashamed. Something happened that you couldn't really control, and you're feeling bad about it. You know what we're talking about—wet dreams.

Medically, wet dreams are referred to as "nocturnal emissions." If you've ever woken up from a vivid sexual dream to find a wet spot in your shorts, guess what? You're not alone. This happens to nearly every man during their teen years and follows them all the way into adulthood.

While women may not physically respond to sexual dreams the exact same way men do, they do have them. Does this mean you're bad or sinful? Does having a dream that's beyond your control cause God to turn away from you? The emphatic answer to both questions is, "No!"

Having a wet dream doesn't mean you are evil; it means you are a human.

Men, there are two primary reasons you are having wet dreams:

1. **You have raging hormones.**

    Do you remember when you started growing hair in weird places and your voice started squeaking all the time? It's called puberty, and everyone faces it!

    Merriam-Webster's Dictionary simply defines "puberty" as, *"the period of life when a person's sexual organs mature, and he or she becomes able to have children."*[1]

    During the maturing process, the body begins making a hormone called testosterone. At this point, men are able to release sperm. Over time, if your body cannot find a way to release sperm, it starts looking for an out. This is where wet dreams come in. By wet dreams, your body is able to get rid of the sperm which has been built up from a lack of release. While this is most common among teenagers and those in their early twenties, it can happen to men of any age once they've gone through puberty.

    However, when you get married and become sexually active, you will likely find this experience happening less and less. In the meantime,

---

[1] http://www.learnersdictionary.com/definition/puberty.

don't sweat it. It's just your body's way of doing its business. In this case, we see no need to repent.

2. **You have real desires.**

Let's face it. Men are visual. But, this doesn't excuse poor behavior, nor does it excuse a man entertaining provocative thoughts in his mind. Nonetheless, the truth remains: Men tend to be more susceptible to what they see. This means that every day is a battle for most guys in our society. From scandalous commercials to under-dressed strangers, more than most realize, men have to fight off lust every time they turn around.

When so much of your day is spent combating provocative ideas or images, it's inevitable that sexual thoughts will make their way into your dreams. If you are having sexual dreams at night, it may be because you are fighting it so stringently during the day. As a Christian, you cannot afford to allow lustful thoughts to reside in your mind, but neither can you avoid them. If you are fighting, stand strong! The grace of God is sufficient!

On the other hand, if you are having wet dreams as a result of a poor decision you made while you were conscious, then you do need to repent. Flooding your mind with sexual thoughts during the day is certain to lead to sexual dreams at night.

Keep your mind out of the gutter!

You were made for more.

Ultimately, we cannot be the ones to answer whether or not you need to repent for the dreams you have had. God is the One looking at your heart, not us.

So, here's our final piece of advice: If you are questioning yourself as to whether or not you need to repent, there is an old adage that fits nicely here: "It's better to be safe than sorry."

It's never a bad idea to ask God to cleanse you of iniquity. We are not, by any means, suggesting that you need to live in fear or condemnation every time you have a wet dream. Yet, we do want to encourage you to remember that God honors those who seek to live in purity and holiness. By His grace, you have what it takes to travel the narrow way with strength and stability!

46

IF I KNOW I'VE FOUND "THE ONE," IS SEX OK?

Let's not kid ourselves. When you've found the person you want to spend the rest of your life with, you're eager to share everything you have with them—including your body.

We've discovered this doesn't get easier the longer you date. As a matter of fact, the closer we got to saying, "I do," the more intentional we had to become about staying pure.

To answer the question plain and simple: No, it's not ok to go further because you are dating the person you plan to one day marry.

Here are the three primary reasons why:

1. **Sometimes plans change.**

    We're not trying to ruin your party, but the reality is you could be wrong. You may wake up three months from now thinking, "Am I crazy? I can't marry this person!" Pamela Paul noted on her article for *Time* magazine that 20% of engagements are called off before the wedding.[1] That's two out of every ten engagements that come to a screeching halt, not including "serious" relationships that ended before a proposal was even made.

If you give in now, what happens if things change later? You will face the regret of wishing you had waited to give yourself solely to your future husband or wife.

2. If it's that serious, get married.

If you're certain you're with the person you are supposed to marry, stop waiting and go for it! Don't try to fight an unnecessary battle. If you have the blessing of your parents and spiritual leaders then why hold back? Paul wrote:

> *"It's better to marry than to burn with lust."*
>
> 1 Corinthians 7:9 (NLT)

If you're battling sexual temptation with the person you are positive you are supposed to marry, the solution is not to give into impurity;

---

[1] *Time*. "Calling it Off." Pamela Paul. http://www.time.com. Oct. 1, 2003.

it might very well be to just get married. Hey, we're just echoing the apostle Paul!

3. **It doesn't change the Bible.**

    We saved the best for last. Above every other reason, as a believer, you should save sex for marriage simply on the basis of scripture. In his letter to the church of Corinth, Paul warns his readers to flee from sexual immorality. God will not ignore sexual impurity just because you plan to one day marry the person you're dating. As we've already said, we know that sex is more tempting and seemingly more justifiable the closer you get to marriage; but it is not acceptable until you've come together in holy matrimony.

If you are reading this and are battling the fires of temptation, just know you are not alone. More people than you'll ever realize fight exactly what you are fighting right now. Some of the Bible's greatest men fought this exact temptation. While you cannot excuse nor justify sin, you can find peace in knowing that you aren't the only one who has ever walked this road.

We challenge you to pray about these points and really consider why going further with the person you plan to marry is still off limits. It may seem insurmountable during this phase of your relationship, but if you fight for purity now, you can live free of regret later.

47

IS IT OK TO LIVE TOGETHER BEFORE MARRIAGE?

Every time this question is asked, there is someone who wants to get technical. Could you technically live together without crossing sexual lines? Sure, but you have a better chance of winning the lottery. This isn't a matter of what you can or cannot do. The real issue you need to consider is what shacking up will cost you.

Here are the top four things you sacrifice when you choose to live together before marriage:

1. **You sacrifice longevity.**

    We've got some bad news. The odds are not in your favor if you're shacking up. Research suggests that those in a dating relationship who live together prior to marriage are 50% to 80% more likely to divorce than those who wait until marriage to live together.[1] The last thing we need

---

1 http://www.focusonthefamily.com/marriage/preparing-for-marriage/test-driving-marriage/maier-on-cohabitation

is another family unit torn apart by divorce. Do you want a "happily ever after" marriage? Well, if you're living under the same roof right now, it's probably not going to happen.

In the words of John Maxwell, you can either "pay now, play later" or "play now, pay later." It might seem innocent and harmless, but statistics say you're headed for a train wreck. Pay the price. Otherwise, you're setting yourself up for a pretty grim future.

2. You sacrifice purity.

Nothing good happens behind closed doors—unless you're married, of course! So, here's the deal. When it comes to sex, good intentions quickly fade when no one's looking. Do you think you could live with your date without crossing a line?

Give us a break!

Have you ever heard the phrase, "Curiosity killed the cat?" Well, that's not all curiosity kills; it also kills relationships.

Your home is meant to be a safe place, somewhere you can let your guard down. If you and your date are at "home," it only takes one weak moment, where you both let your guard down, for sexual sin to creep in. If you're living together and trying to stay pure, you're playing with fire. And unless someone moves out, you'll both get burnt sooner or later.

3. You sacrifice credibility.

In the world of social networking, you are bound to see some bizarre things. For example, a few years ago, we were browsing around and ran across a girl we went to high school with. Come to find out, after graduating college, she got involved with a few ministries and did a lot of missionary work. Later, she decided to settle down here in the States and focus on ministering within the local church. We would often see her making inspirational posts, challenging people to follow Jesus.

There was just one major problem.

She would also make posts about her living with her boyfriend. With us, that killed all her credibility—and probably did for others, too.

If you want to be significant in God's kingdom, you must live by God's commands. Living under the same roof was meant for marriage.

4. You sacrifice celebration.

A while back, a family member got married who had lived with his girlfriend for nearly two years before popping the question. When the wedding day rolled around, someone asked the groom if he was excited about the honeymoon. His response baffled us all. He said, "It's just another vacation to me."

Just another vacation?

Are you serious?

Because we valued each other's sexual purity and chose to wait, we were ecstatic about our honeymoon! We dreamed of the day we could fully give ourselves to each other. So, for us, the consummation of our marriage was an incredible celebration.

We've heard many people, who chose to live together while dating, say that marriage is just a piece of paper or a mere legal bond. If you don't wait until you've tied the knot to live together, you'll most likely approach your wedding day and honeymoon with the same sad mentality—and it'll be anything but an exciting celebration.

We hope you will take these points to heart. If you and your date have already moved in with each other, make a change as quickly as you can! It may be a little challenging, but you have what it takes to right your wrongs. If you really care for them and want a bright future, it's worth the wait.

48

HOW CAN MY DATE AND I STAY SEXUALLY PURE

There are a million different things you can do to maintain purity in a relationship. Before we were married, everyone wanted to give us their two-cents worth on what does and doesn't work prior to marriage. While much of the advice we were given helped tremendously, some of it was simply too much.

Our goal isn't to make you feel like you have to live bogged down by some unattainable standard; our goal here is that you would be able to uphold purity no matter what you face. We chose the top ten things that worked for us, which you and your date can immediately implement to stay on the right track.

1. **Have a list of non-negotiables.**

    Everybody needs a list of non-negotiables in their life. What you *will not* do is just as important to your success as what you *will* do. A list of non-negotiables consists of things you've already predetermined to refrain from.

While we were teaching this series at our church, a young lady who was in a serious relationship came up to us afterwards and told us a few of her non-negotiables. At the time we were teaching this series, summer was full on and pool days were in full swing. One of her non-negotiables was that her boyfriend would not see her in a bathing suit until they were married, should their relationship progress. This is an awesome example of a non-negotiable.

2. **Avoid sexually provocative entertainment—like a plague!**

Have you ever watched a cooking show? Maybe you've seen an episode of *Man vs. Food*. If you have, then you know that even when your stomach is full, there's something about these shows that makes you want to eat. The way the food is described, the imagery—it all adds up, causing you to want what they're presenting. So, even when you're completely full, watching just one episode can stir up a big appetite.

The same is true with sexual entertainment. Whether it's a song or a TV show, sexually provocative entertainment is never a good idea. Next time you are watching a movie with your date and a steamy love scene comes on the screen, get out of there or turn it off. A sexual scene can inspire a sexual thought, which could easily lead to a sexual action. This tip is key for anyone who wants to keep their relationship on the right track.

3. **Keep the lights on.**

   When it comes to relationships, nothing good ever happens in the dark—unless, of course, you're married. While it's certainly tempting to cut off the lights and enjoy the evening, if you value your purity, you must fight the urge.

   Like it or not, our actions are affected by the atmosphere we are in, more so than we realize. A romantic setting only leads to romantic decisions. And unless you've put a ring on it and said, "I do," that's off-limits. Keep the lights on!

4. **Watch your mouth.**

   While it is healthy to make sure the person you're dating knows that you're physically attracted to them, you must guard against it ever going past that point. Physical attraction and sexual attraction are not the same thing. To admire and verbalize your appreciation for someone's physical appearance is one thing, but verbalizing sexual attraction and desire is quite different.

Over time and as your relationship progresses, you will find it becomes easier to excuse sexual innuendos because they're made by someone you have grown comfortable with. However, comfortable or not, sexual talk before marriage is way too dangerous. Impurity doesn't start with your actions; it starts with your thoughts and words.

5. Granny panties, maybe?

Are we suggesting you raid your grandma's dresser and borrow a pair of her ugly, old panties? Maybe so. If you would be too embarrassed to undress because of them, why not? Could you imagine how awkward it would be if, right as you were about to cross the line, you had to stop and explain why you were wearing panties that looked like a diaper and smelled like mothballs?

Awkward!

Here's the point. Sometimes, the war for your purity can get pretty intense. Trust us; we've been there. In the heat of the moment, you are not in your right mind. Emotions are flaring, desires are escalating, and you are liable to do something you'll regret. We aren't necessarily suggesting you steal from your granny's dresser, cause that's kind of creepy—unless, of course, it would really help!

What we *are* suggesting is that you be proactive in fighting impurity. Don't wait until you are in the heat of the moment to try to make a quality decision. Sometimes the only way to fight extreme temptation is with extreme precautions.

6. **No downtime.**

When you have nothing to do, chances are you will do the wrong thing. Thankfully, we had a mentor who helped us avoid this disaster in our dating days.

As we were leaving church one Friday night he asked us, "You guys have any plans this weekend?" Casually, we responded, "Yeah, we're probably just going to get together and hangout." His face dropped as though we'd spoken profanities in the church sanctuary.

"What? Is something wrong?" we asked. He said, "Yeah, something's wrong! If you're getting together without a plan, you're just asking for trouble." He went on to explain the dangers of downtime in dating. From that point on, we were very intentional about making sure our time together had a purpose and a plan. If you are going to maintain your purity, you had better do the same.

7. **No provocative pictures.**

   With all the social media platforms online today, this one is huge. There has never been a time when making the wrong decision has been easier than it is today. Sending provocative pictures to your date is not only dangerous, in many cases, it is also illegal—not to mention the fact that once it's in cyberspace, anything can happen to it! A lot of image-based social networks give their users the idea that every post is completely private and that using their website or app bears no consequence.

   Newsflash: EVERY image bears a consequence and, technically, is never totally private. However, even if no one other than your date sees these provocative images, you've still violated the standard of sexual purity that we, as Christians, are called to follow.

   It may seem irrational now, but what if you and your date made a pledge together that neither of you would send any type of photo to one another until marriage? Sounds extreme, but you are worth it!

8. **Whatever you do, don't lie down.**

   Relaxation leads to vulnerability. Inside of marriage, this is awesome. You can kick back, release the stress of the day, and let your guard down. Did you catch that last part? In dating, that's where you can easily get tripped up. When you let your guard down, you open the door for your desires to run wild. Then, if you get too relaxed, one thing can lead to another; and before you know it, temptation is pounding on your door.

So, don't put yourself in such a vulnerable position. The momentary satisfaction you'll find snuggled up together isn't worth what it could lead to.

Our advice? Relax alone. Your purity is more important than your rest. Don't ever lie down together!

9. Going under cover? Don't!

It's movie night! You're next to your honey with a bucket of warm, buttery popcorn and an ice cold drink. There's only one thing missing—a nice, cozy blanket. Sounds perfect, huh?

Not so fast!

If you are sharing a blanket on movie night, the movie will quickly lose your attention—that, you can be sure of! If it's chilly, change the thermostat. In dating, nothing good goes on underneath the covers. Save that for marriage! To avoid a bunch of regret from getting too touchy, feely during the movie, ditch the covers!

10. Run for your life!

We had several moments, while dating, where we got dangerously close to crossing the line. You know, when you just happen to show up and there's no one else home or a hug that felt too good to let go.

The list goes on and on.

What should you do when you find the moment getting the best of you?

You do "The Forrest Gump" and take off running. If you find yourself in a position you didn't intend to be in, get as far away as you can, as quickly as you can. Don't worry about giving an explanation. Don't even worry about trying to be nice. Just get out of there! You can explain later, if necessary. What matters most in this situation is that you do whatever it takes to guard your purity. So, "Run, Forrest, run!"

These ten principles are a strong start for any couple endeavoring to remain pure sexually in their relationship. We challenge you to apply these dating principles, and do it the right way!

49

DO I NEED AN ACCOUNTABILITY PARTNER?

This is one of the most essential ingredients of success in keeping your dating relationship pure.

In Ecclesiastes 4:9-10 (NKJV), King Solomon wrote, *"Two are better than one,"* and that, *". . . if they fall, one will lift up his companion. But woe to him who is alone when he falls, for he has no one to help him up."*

In our world, it's not a matter of "if" you will be challenged with sexual promiscuity; it's a matter of "when." Despite the challenge, we firmly believe you have what it takes to fight and win!

The secret to living pure is keeping no secrets. That's where an accountability partner comes in. Do you have someone you can talk to regularly, openly, and honestly? If not, it's time to find someone! There are three things every accountability partner must be able to do:

1. **They must be able to show compassion.**

    "Be happy with those who are happy, and weep with those who weep."

    Romans 12:15 (NLT)

   In pursuing a life of purity, you are certain to have ups and downs. The last thing you need, when you feel like you've blown it, is an egotistical accountability partner who can't sympathize with you. Look for a leader who hurts when you hurt and rejoices when you rejoice.

   While peers are important, we highly recommend finding an accountability partner who's older, even if just by a few years—and here's why.

   Typically, they are a few steps ahead of you and have probably already been through the same struggles you are facing. If you find that your accountability partner can't ever seem to relate to your struggles, you need to find someone else who can, to assume that role. A good accountability partner is one who can see where you're at and understand what you're facing.

2. **They must be able to give correction.**

    "If your brother or sister sins, go and point out their fault, just between the two of

you. If they listen to you, you have won them over."

Matthew 18:15 (NIV)

This is the least appealing, yet the most beneficial part of having a good accountability partner. Let's be honest, sometimes the truth hurts. No one enjoys correction. It's painful!

Lieutenant General Chesty Puller has been credited for the old saying: "Pain is weakness leaving the body." This statement can certainly be applied to one's pursuit of purity!

Look, with a good accountability partner, you will face moments that feel almost unbearable. They will say things that make you squirm, but you need someone in your life who makes your palms a little sweaty, someone who you could never look in the eyes and lie to.

Who do you have in your life that fills this description? If someone doesn't immediately come to mind, for the sake of your purity, you had better get to looking!

3. They must be able to keep things confidential.

A gossip goes around telling secrets, but those who are trustworthy can keep a confidence."

Proverbs 11:13 (NLT)

Shouldn't we all live with nothing to hide and nothing to prove? Yes, but everyone falls while they are learning to walk. It's no different in the fight of purity. Regardless how far you've already gone or what you are currently struggling with, the greatest way to win the battle you are fighting in the dark is to bring it into the light. The only way to do this is by talking to someone.

As long as you conceal your struggle, you will have to fight the battle alone. Find someone of Godly character and integrity to be your accountability partner. You do not want someone in this position who will broadcast your weaknesses and mistakes to the world. Look for an individual who has a genuine "your secret is safe with me" mentality, and you'll find that few things prove to be more beneficial on this journey.

Purity ultimately boils down to planning ahead. Unless you set up safety parameters in your life, an accident is almost inevitable. By submitting yourself to the evaluation of another, you are setting yourself up for success. That's why you need an accountability partner.

Take these three principles and find someone who can help you steer clear of jeopardizing your purity!

WILL GOD REALLY BLESS MY SEX LIFE IF I WAIT UNTIL MARRIAGE TO HAVE SEX?

In our early dating years, we heard countless ministers at abstinence seminars tell us that God would bless our sex life when we got married if we would remain pure while dating. Thankfully, even though it was one of the greatest struggles we have ever faced, we were able to give ourselves to each other on our wedding night for the first time. It was incredible!

Has God blessed our sex life? Yes, absolutely! Did our years of fighting for purity cause God to give us a little something extra that He doesn't give to those who messed up before marriage? Honestly, we don't know. We don't believe that God sits in heaven, looking at one couple and says, "They waited, so I will bless them to have really good sex," and then looks at another couple and says, "They didn't wait; therefore, I decree they will be subjected to mediocre sex all of their days."

Does this mean you can have sex now without it affecting your future? Absolutely not. We actually believe the exact opposite. What you do with someone sexually outside of marriage could complicate things in your life for years to come.

If you aren't married, but you are sexually active, there are three things you could easily end up struggling with in the future:

1. **Comparison.**

    If you are sleeping around while single, you will no doubt carry memories of those sexual experiences into your marriage. Such memories can easily become the measuring rod for all sexual activities shared between you and your future spouse.

    This can be a catastrophic problem! It's not fair to you or them.

    The same principle is true when either person in a relationship carries a history of pornography into the bedroom. If you compare your spouse with the person you were sexually involved with during your past, you are setting your relationship up for failure. Your sexual involvement may seem quite innocent at the moment, but when your wedding day comes, you will be shocked to find that your past actions have costly and dangerous side effects. Our advice? Stay innocent.

2. Condemnation.

One of the most common things we hear from those who have battled with sexual sin prior to marriage is how much they wish they never would have given themselves to anyone other than their spouse. They spend countless hours regretting the mistakes of their past.

Condemnation can be deadly. It traps you in the past and leaves you feeling helpless. Inside a marriage, few things could be more damaging. How are you supposed to move forward when your mind is constantly re-living past wrongs? Do you want to fight such thoughts every single time you and your future spouse start to get intimate? To avoid this obstacle, you must get passionate about avoiding sexual sin.

3. Confidence.

If you have been sexually active, your future spouse may feel as though they have to compete with your past experiences. This means that while you are battling with comparison, they are battling with confidence. What you do today could be setting up your future husband or wife for insecurities tomorrow. We hope you see that your sexual decisions cannot be made lightly.

When you get married, do you want your spouse riddled with a lack of confidence, fighting off thoughts like, "I wonder if they enjoy me more than they enjoyed their ex?"

Of course not!

Sadly, these thoughts are often present among couples who had sex outside of marriage. If you care about your future spouse's self-esteem and confidence, make sure your decisions today are ones they will be proud of tomorrow.

We know this isn't the easiest subject to address. Though it can be difficult, the joy of saving yourself for your spouse is knowing you can enter into your sex life without comparison or condemnation, which ultimately allows your future spouse to be who they are with confidence and security.

If you're reading this and are thinking, "It's too late for me. I've already blown it," not so fast! We have good news and bad news.

Let's start with the bad news first. You cannot press the rewind button and redo yesterday.

The good news?

You don't need to. You may not be able to change yesterday, but you can change today. There is only one solution to all of these issues:

His name is Jesus.

When you go to Him in humility and repentance, He will gladly lead you into a place of restoration and redemption.

If you are fighting these things, connect with a spiritual advisor, such as your pastor, who can help you begin the healing process. Don't waste any time. Make a move today!

C

CONCLUSION

Now, more than ever before, we need an awakening. We need a generation who will stand in opposition to the ways of today's culture. We need men and women who will not bow down to the social norm.

The impact made by your stand for sexual purity reaches far beyond the benefits you will reap in your own life. It reaches into the lives of others as a testimony, a living sign that purity can be attained no matter how difficult the struggle may be.

Our prayer is that the principles you have learned in this book will aid you along your journey. In Christ, it matters not whether you are standing on top of the highest mountain or trembling in the lowest valley; His grace is sufficient! You can live a life that is pleasing to Him. While you will no doubt face rough patches along the way, we firmly believe you can make it to your destination intact, missing nothing, wholly complete. Some might still be saying, "But what if

I've already gone too far?" Again, we say that your mistakes are not beyond the reach of Jesus' love for you and His mercy towards you. All you have to do is repent, cry out to God for mercy, and walk in His grace, as He restores all that has been lost. With Christ, you are never too far gone.

Do not limit the principles you have learned in this book to mere information that only impacts you personally. Impart what you have discovered into the lives of those around you. The world is aching for individuals who will stand for holiness and righteousness. Your commitment to purity is just what they are looking for. Show them that they do not have to live at the mercy of corrupt, fleshly desires. Instead, they can by the power of the Holy Spirit say, "Yes," to the narrow way. Be bold and courageous. You can lead them to a life of integrity and wholeness.

The apostle Paul wrote this about God's grace:

> "... where sin increased, grace abounded all the more."
>
> Romans 5:20 (ESV)

God has always had a plan when it looked as though wickedness was overtaking the world. When darkness is on the rise, you can rest assured that the plan of heaven is to overwhelm the darkness with light. You are a part of Heaven's plan for this hour. As you live among those whose lives are abounding with sin, be an expression of God's grace that abounds all the more. The light shining from a holy remnant can penetrate the darkness of this generation. Let your life and your relationships shine with the light of purity and holiness, as you approach the issues of dating and sex.

Together, we can start a revolution in the realm of purity.

www.ingramcontent.com/pod-product-compliance
Lightning Source LLC
Chambersburg PA
CBHW051938290426
44110CB00015B/2030